A WRITER BY ACCIDENT

Some priest-friends t(I presented *At the coal face: recollections of a*
city and country priest   o jokingly chided me for writing a book,
the content of which wa   k and no play'. This prompted me to publish this ancillary volume   ny years I have derived considerable satisfaction from writing a   ishing, and much enjoyment from my
acquaintance, association   idship with scribblers like myself.

In connection with th   ition of this book I wish to thank all who
helped to ensure its accur   irticular: Cara Trant of the Kerry Literary
and Cultural Centre, who   me the entire set of the programmes of
Listowel's Writer's Week; l   en Synon, who checked the chapter on
her father; Arthur Flynn, v   me access to the minutes of Irish P.E.N.
from 1972 to the present; T   Hussey and Superintendent John Mee for
information on the mem(Jeremiah Mee at Glenamaddy; Thomas
Armitage, Michael Costell(Pádraig de Brún for details on the Kerry
Archaeological and Histori   ety; Mona O'Donnell for making available records of the beginnii   progress of the Canon Sheehan Literary
Society; William Hallihan a   s Ina Lillis for their recollections of the
North Cork Writers Festiva   Dónal Ó Luanaigh for the history of the
early years of the National l   y of Ireland Society.

Apart from writing and j   ling, I have enjoyed foreign travel. In that
regard I wish to express my   ude to the staff of the Bon Voyage Travel
Agency who arranged the d   of many of my trips abroad. I am indebted to Matthew Kennelly, an   iephew John, who ensured the accuracy
of my recollections of earlier   with the Listowel Boy Scouts.

Thanks are due to Fr N   irber, SJ, Stephen Collins, Mgr Martin
Cummins, Canon Patrick J.   n, Fr Francis Mitchell, Helen Murray,
Maurice O'Connell and Fr S   Toohey for helpful criticism.

I am grateful to Mrs Eileer   s for preparing the manuscript for publication.

I am delighted to have the   ord provided by Conor Brady.

ITHONY GAUGHAN, *1 July 2002*

To
the members of the organising committee who contribute
so much to the success of Writers' Week, Listowel

CONTENTS

FOREWORD

'A Writer by Accident' thus Fr J. Anthony Gaughan describes himself in the title of this remarkable autobiography. When he first committed his life to the priesthood, Tony Gaughan had no way of knowing that the role of prolific author also lay ahead of him. But if his writing *persona* came about by 'accident' it has surely been a joyous and beneficial mishap for the world of Irish letters.

I first encountered Tony Gaughan through a mutual interest in the history of Irish policing. I had completed my postgraduate thesis at UCD on *Law Enforcement and Security Policy in the Irish Free State 1922-1932* and Tony was researching for his book *Memoirs of Constable Jeremiah Mee, RIC*. I was planning to turn out a version of my thesis as *Guardians of the Peace* (the first history of the Garda Síochána) when my inquiries led me to the door of this most energised priest-writer.

My information needs were modest. In order to narrate the context in which the Garda had been established, I had to describe something of the predecessor force, the Royal Irish Constabulary. Primary sources were few. But Tony had the confidence of the Mee family whose father, Jeremiah, had led the police revolt in Listowel barracks during the War of Independence. He had access to good written sources. Tony also had (like myself) family connections in the old RIC.

Turning to Tony for help, I was deluged with information. I was left with an abiding recollection of his generosity, enthusiasm and the sense of collegiality which he instinctively felt for another researcher/writer. Photostats came in the post. Telephone calls came with some new gem of information. Notes were dropped in the letterbox while I was out. My only regret was that limitations of space allowed me to utilise only a fraction of the information which he so generously and diligently searched out for me.

This was in the relatively early stages of his development as a writer. Jeremiah Mee's *Memoirs* were to be followed in time by a succession of publications, ranging far and wide across the landscape of recent Irish history and sociology.

In time, a clear and distinctive pattern could be discerned in his work – his own *genre*. Tony's specialisation was to be in the byways, focusing often on the lesser-known figures and events whose significance is often overlooked in the conventional treatment of Irish history.

Hence he wrote of Constable Mee, an individual whose name does not appear in the history books but whose *démarche* was a pivotal event in the War of Independence. He wrote of Austin Stack, the influential but rarely remembered Kerry patriot. He wrote of Dr Alfie O'Rahilly, one of the most colourful individuals to have lived in twentieth century Ireland but hardly a household name outside Cork and Munster. Tony had an instinctive understanding of the way in which lesser known players and less recorded events feed into the greater sweep of history, often changing its course.

Time and again, his work gravitates back towards his beloved Listowel and towards County Kerry. Little wonder that when Listowel Writers', Week was inaugurated, Father Anthony Gaughan was a central figure in the project. And, as it has matured in excellence over the years, he has remained one of its sheet-anchors.

If Tony Gaughan's name is inextricably linked with Listowel Writers', Week it is, of course, synonymous with Irish P.E.N. The life of the writer is often difficult. It can be a solitary existence. The support, companionship and guidance of fellow-practitioners can be crucially important, whether in times of success or otherwise. Tony Gaughan has been one the driving influences of Irish P.E.N. for many years. In a sense, it has become his second 'parish' and his flock has come to rely on his instincts of care, his professionalism and, of course, his sense of fun and sociability. I had the honour of his invitation, shortly after I was appointed editor of *The Irish Times*, to deliver an address at the organisation's annual dinner. I have the happiest recollection – with my wife, Ann – of a memorable evening in Dalkey, and of the esteem and affection in which his fellow-writers held their chairman.

The pages of this autobiography abound with fascinating people and memorable encounters. But they are also replete with practical advice to those whose lives in whole or in part are bound up with writing. There are surprises on every page and in every chapter. It is a *tour d'horizon* of the Irish writing world from a unique perspective. Read on – and enjoy the story of a full life.

CONOR BRADY, *1 June 2002*

CHAPTER I

The town of the three Ss

I was born in Listowel in 1932. Like most of my fellow-townspeople mine was only a second-generation Listowel family. My grandfather, John Broderick (known as John Broder/Bruaidair before moving into the town) was born in 1863 into a large family on a small farm at Gortdromagowna in the parish of Moyvane/Knockanure. His father, Danny Broder/Broderick, died in 1911, aged 94, and his grandfather, known as 'Big Dan' of Lisroe, near Duagh, died aged 97. My grandfather established a drapery business at the bottom of Church (now Ashe) Street, near the Small Square, and married Elizabeth (Lizzie) O'Brien of Ballylongford. In 1907 he built a house at the top of Church Street (now replaced by the Listowel Credit Union Building) and in the bottom floor ran a public-house until he died in 1933.

John Broderick had one son and three daughters. The son Mike who was born in 1892 completed his education in St Michael's College in 1910. As he had little prospects of decent employment he set out to try his fortune in the US. He went to California where relatives belonging to his mother's family were already settled. Like millions of others he found himself out of work during the depression. At the end of that bleak period he arrived in Chicago and found employment as a clerk in the Chicago Power Company. His relief at having secure employment and memories of the depression persuaded him to stay in that job until he retired. Like his father he was apolitical and, unlike most of his friends, played no part in the Democratic ward politics of the city. He married, raised a family and never returned to his homeland.

John Broderick's oldest daughter, Bridget, was born in 1893. She married Tom Shanahan in 1922. A veteran of the war of independence, he was an admirer of Michael Collins, supported the treaty and joined the Irish Free State army. He was reported for releasing one of his erstwhile comrades at the beginning of the civil war and was transferred to the Curragh Camp, where he spent the rest of his military service apart from a posting in the Kilkenny-Wexford area in 1940-1 during the emergency. During the early most critical phase of the civil war he was in charge of the detail accompanying President William T. Cosgrave from the Curragh Camp to meetings of the Provisional government in Dublin, a fact appreciated and never forgotten by the Cosgrave family. From his return to North Kerry in 1942 until 1969 he resided in the house in Listowel built by my grandfather and conducted a number of businesses including a public-house and a garage.

Catherine, the next daughter, was born in 1894. She married Anthony Gaughan in 1930. He was one of the large family of Sergeant Anthony Gaughan who retired from the Royal Irish Constabulary in April 1916. After leaving Summerhill College, Sligo, Anthony Gaughan was a clerk in the Great Northern Railway in Portadown and later in Drogheda. On its establishment he joined the Irish Free State army as a lieutenant and until he left the service was stationed in the Curragh Camp. Subsequently he was in charge of the Labour Exchange in Passage West, County Cork.

John Broderick's third daughter, Elizabeth (Lizzie) was born in 1896. A tom-boy who liked to play football with her male contemporaries and who was followed everywhere by a large dog, she died in 1924, aged 28. Her early death followed a traumatic experience in 1921 when she witnessed the assassination of District Inspector Tobias O'Sullivan, R.I.C. She was taken to the headquarters of the crown forces in Tralee but after a day-long interrogation did not disclose the name of one of the attackers whom she had recognised. Subsequently four innocent local men were convicted by a drumhead court-martial for the assassination. Two of these were to hang and their lives were saved only by the fact that the Anglo-Irish truce was formally declared twenty-four hours before the time fixed for the execution. One of the two, a local carpenter, named Jacko Lenihan, was wont to vividly recall his close brush with the hangman while showing the formal communication he had received from the authorities indicating the time and place of his execution.

Ours was a pro-treaty family. I recall vividly being frequently told by my mother and aunt of how upset their father was when reading in the *Irish Independent* reports of inflammatory remarks by de Valera at public meetings in March 1922. Nor did the anti-treatyites endear themselves to the family when about 150 of them took control of the town in May and June of that year. They billeted themselves in local houses, including my grandfather's, where a group of them occupied the top floor for almost two months. In addition, they commandeered food, drink and other goods from shops and at gun-point took £1,658 from the local branch of the National Bank in the name of the 'Republican Army'. These experiences and their feelings of devastation at the assassination of Michael Collins caused the family to be most partisan with regard to Party politics. As I grew older I tended to change my voting preferences and to vote in general elections for a change of government but this was not something of which they ever approved.

I received my primary education in three different counties: Junior Infants and 5th and 6th class in Listowel National School; Senior Infants, 2nd, 3rd and 4th class in Sisters of Mercy Convent School and National School in Passage West, County Cork; and 1st class in the national school at Ballyshannon, Kilcullen, County Kildare. This was due to my parents' troubled marriage which in turn was occasioned largely by my father having a serious drink problem.

From 1945 to 1950 I attended St Michael's College, Listowel. This sister college to St. Brendan's Seminary in Killarney was established in 1879. Fr Arthur Moynihan, administrator, Listowel parish 1878-82, and Bishop Daniel McCarthy were the prime movers behind its establishment.

In the 1940s St Michael's had six teachers, including the president, Canon David O'Connor, and 120 students. Latin and Greek constituted the core of the curriculum. Employment prospects in the area were bleak. As a result there was a single-minded emphasis on success in public examinations which could deliver scholarships to university, the acquisition of posts in the civil service as clerical or junior executive officers, admission to the teacher-training college or the Garda training centre. But apart from orchestrating this emphasis parents, having a keen appreciation of its importance, were eager that their children would benefit from a secondary education.

St Michael's was a fee-paying college. However, the fees were not much more than nominal. And no boy was ever refused admission or attendance for not being able to pay the fees. One result arising from this was that, owing to the college's limited resources, no provision could be made for games, other than Canon David O'Connor personally purchasing two footballs each year for the juniors and seniors to kick around during lunch hour!

The college had its usual complement of characters. By far the most popular one was Mícheál Quigley. Even at the age of 15 he was well over six feet and built accordingly. He was easy-going and had an infectious smile. Mícheál downed a pint at one of the local bars each evening on his way up to study at 5 o'clock. Generally he was involved in the pranks which went on. But invariably with outrageous effrontery he would talk himself out of any tight corner. Of considerable ability he refused to be caught up in the academic rat-race that was St Michael's. He qualified as a radio officer and sailed through life with the same relaxed attitude which he had at college.

While Mícheál Quigley was the most popular character at St

Michael's Johneen Keane was the outstanding one. As I disliked nicknames I always knew him and referred to him as John. Although more than four years his junior we have been life-long friends from our earliest years. With the other boys of Church Street we roamed the town and its neighbourhood, especially Gurtinard Wood and the banks of the Feale. John was Listowel's answer to the William of Richmal Crompton's delightful series of boyhood adventure stories. He was full of energy, with a lively intelligence and at the foot of most of the mischief in which the Church Street boys became involved. John enjoyed putting on little concerts. These would be held either in the hay-shed behind the premises of Mick Regan, the harness-maker, at the top of Church Street, or more grandly in the hall on the top floor of the Carnegie library. There would be no adult involvement. John would be the organiser, MC and would write a sketch or two for the show. He also prepared the posters. Even then he had a penchant for what is now known as the 'sound bite'. One of our pals, Willie Regan, was able to play a few tunes on a violin. I recall at the top of one of John's posters: 'Will Regan play the fiddle?'

In my second year at St Michaels I found myself in the same senior study hall as John. His progress through the college had been eventful. Apart from English and Irish he had shown little interest in most other subjects. As he advanced through St Michael's the relationship between John and the teachers was an uneasy one. Besides he remained as lively and thrusting as ever and was at the centre of any prank which was going on. This resulted in his expulsion on not a few occasions, not verbally but physically by Canon David O'Connor, a human Mount Vesuvius, if ever there was one. After representations were made to him, Canon David would permit John to return to the college, where the rest of us would welcome him back like an all-conquering hero! At this stage John was showing unmistakeable signs of literary talent. While the rest of us were filling our exercise books with tortuously produced English and Irish essays John's contained poems in English and Irish written by himself. He was also generous in helping those of us who were struggling to produce essays in Irish not vitiated by an inordinate number of grammatical errors. Occasionally he would request a small fee for this service!

My friendship with John was bonded by our enthusiasm for Gaelic football. We were the centre-field pairing for the Thomas Ashes team, one of the three teams which annually contested the Listowel Town League. We also played together on the town's senior team, the Emmets, in the North Kerry League. I was always glad to be playing on the same team as John. As a friend of mine who was marking him in a football match complained to me on one occasion: 'Johneen is all elbows and a bit of a nettle'.

An incident in a football match cast a shadow over our friendship for three years. I was refereeing a Town League match. During the course of it my attention was drawn to John. Frequently John has amused interviewers by telling them that one of his hobbies is cloud-watching. In this instance he was not so engaged. He and an opposing player were embroiled in each other, while play continued at the other end of the field. All I saw was the two of them flailing at each other. I ordered them off the field. Jack Quille, the other player, soon came to terms with the situation. John continued a protest which extended to his refusing to speak to me for three years. Ever since then as he invariably and jokingly reminds me although he has forgiven me he has not forgotten the incident!

During a visit home in the autumn of 1959 I enquired of John (Chuck) Roche, a local wit, what was new in the town. 'Fr Tony', he said, 'Listowel now is the town of the three Ss, *Sive*, "Shanahans Stamps" and the new superintendent'. After trying his hand at a number of jobs, including a bleak period in Northampton and London, John Keane returned home to Ireland and worked in Doneraile, County Cork, as a chemist's assistant. A year later he transferred to a similar post at Keane-Stack's, Listowel. He married Mary O'Connor from Knocknagoshel and they bought a public house and set up in business. Then after failing to interest the Abbey Theatre in his play *Sive* John asked the Listowel Drama Group to present it. It was tailor-made for them and they entered it in the All-Ireland Theatre Festival then held annually at Athlone. Their success and the subsequent extraordinary popularity of John's other plays were a source of considerable pride to his fellow-townspeople. Indeed, many of us since then have self-consciously basked in the glow of his dramatic and literary achievements. John's break-through with *Sive* was nothing less than an apotheosis. Overnight he became John B. and he was the talk of the town.

The story surrounding Shanahans Stamps Auction Ltd was not one which many Listowel persons enjoyed talking about. In 1954 Paul Singer transferred to Ireland from London, where the Singer family finance business had become bankrupt. He persuaded Jerome Shanahan and his son, Desmond, to transform their auctioneering business in Dún Laoghaire into Shanahans Stamp Auctions Ltd. Having a brilliant mind and a first class third-level education, Singer quickly mastered most aspects of the international trade in philately. He was a consummate publicist and soon great numbers of investors were pouring hundreds of thousands of pounds into 'Shanahans Stamps' on being assured by Singer and Jerome and Desmond Shanahan, his fellow-directors, that the enterprise was one which guaranteed 'profit without risk'. As Singer juggled with huge sums of money this remained so for a few years during which time a £200 stamp auction business became a worldwide-known enterprise valued at five million pounds. Then after a burglary at the firm's premises the company went into receivership and huge amounts of money were never accounted for.

Apart from Singer's intellectual brilliance the initial success of 'Shanahans Stamps' was due to the high regard in which the Shanahans were held by the business community in Dún Laoghaire. The family came from Lixnaw, near Listowel. When 'Shanahans Stamps' appeared to be advancing from success to success Paul Shanahan, a first cousin of Jerome Shanahan, set up an agency for the stamp company in his large boot and shoe shop in Listowel. Hundreds of locals flocked in to invest in 'Shanahans Stamps', including my uncle-in-law, Captain Tom Shanahan, who was also a cousin of the Shanahans from Lixnaw. . When the business failed nearly all of them were left holding worthless 'share certificates'. And later to add insult to injury, owing to incompetence on the part of members of the Irish legal fraternity, Singer walked free, while Desmond Shanahan, who was generally regarded as little more than a dupe in the great scam, had to serve time in prison.

At that time also a new superintendent cast as much gloom over the town as the collapse of 'Shanahans Stamps'. In 1959 the easy-going Tom Mulcahy retired. During his sixteen years in charge of the Listowel Garda District there had been little crime. Most convictions related to cycling at night without a light, allowing animals to stray on the public thoroughfare, farmers neglecting to clear weeds from their land and the occasional row inside or outside a public-house.

Part of Mulcahy's popularity was due to his relaxed attitude to the non-strict observance of closing time in a number of pubs in the town. There were a few of these which were scarcely ever frequented during the day but did 'a roaring trade after hours'. One such was 'Curly Connor's' at the end of Church Street. Here the town's young bloods and not so young bloods gathered almost nightly in Falstaffian revelry. Much of the fun and japes in the town were hatched there. The most memorable was the 'Tom Doodle' charade, mocking politics in general and local Party politics in particular.

Unfortunately another of the escapades associated with 'Curly Connor's' almost coincided with the arrival of the new superintendent. Each summer the members of the local branch of the Pioneer Total Abstinence Association organised an outing. With a fanfare they would set out in one or two buses to tour the Ring of Kerry, the Ring of Cork or visit some other beauty spot. That summer the clientele of 'Curly's' decided to go one better and 'do' both scenic Rings on the Sunday after the Pioneers' outing. They set off and eventually late on the Sunday night found themselves in a small pub between Glengariff and Kenmare. Although they had been liberally imbibing at stops all day long, when they discovered that the stock in the little pub was running out they decided to drink the pub dry: at the time one of the most popular songs was 'The pub with no beer'. They even called in the driver to help to this end. The result was that early on Monday morning neither he nor any of his passengers were in a fit condition to drive. Meanwhile as the hours went by and there was no sign of the excursionists mothers and wives in Listowel were becoming frantic with anxiety and worry. Eventually the bus crawled into the Square after noon on Monday.

Soon afterwards a number of determined ladies met the new superintendent. About a week later 'Curly's' and a few of the other late-night pubs were raided. As usual 'Curly's' was packed. Some of the customers went up through the house in an attempt to avoid arrest. A few solicitors were found in rather humiliating situations. One was poked out of a wardrobe by a Garda and another was told to get out of a bed into which he had jumped fully clothed. The raids continued during the relatively short time the 'new superintendent' served in the town. Although he had quite a few admirers, the late-night drinkers compared his service in the district to the reign of terror during the worst phase of the French Revolution and he was talked about in the town even more than *Sive* or 'Shanahans Stamps'.

CHAPTER 2

A writer by accident

For more than thirty years I have spent much of my free time writing. From this I have derived considerable enjoyment and, most importantly, it has enabled me to meet many interesting persons in Ireland and beyond. While the fact that I was born and raised in Listowel has helped me to be published, I am not aware that this encouraged me to write. In fact I have been a writer by accident. Until 1968 when I was almost 36 years old, it had never occurred to me to write anything for publication.

In the spring of that year I attended a dinner with those who had been ordained with me for the archdiocese of Dublin in 1957. Caomhín de Líon, one of these classmates, presented me with *The Vale of Avoca* which had just been published. His booklet was a fascinating account of Avoca, dealing with the churches, great houses, mineral wealth, traditional industries and biographical sketches of famous native sons, such as Archbishop Daniel Murray of Dublin and

Monsignor John Hagan, rector and founder of the present Irish College in Rome.

A short time earlier I had spent some time in the Doneraile district, near Mallow. I was as fascinated by its historical associations as Caomhín had been by those around Avoca. There was Kilcolman Castle, residence of Edmund Spenser who made the district famous in his epic poem 'The Faerie Queene'. The seat of the much-storied St Leger family was there and was still occupied by Lady Doneraile. John Philpot Curran and Daniel O'Connell, perhaps the two greatest advocates of the Irish bar, enhanced their reputations in cases which originated in the district. Philpot Curran, on behalf of Fr Neale, a local parish priest, conducted a successful prosecution against Lord Doneraile who was required to pay £1,000 damages for an assault on the parish priest. O'Connell was the hero of what became known as the 'Doneraile Conspiracy'. In this case he successfully defended a number of men who had been arraigned for involvement in Whiteboy outrages.

Some distinguished churchmen ministered in the parish of Doneraile. Thomas W. Croke, who served as bishop of Auckland and later as archbishop of Cashel and Emly, was parish priest there from 1866 to 1870. A century and a half before that An tAthair Eoghan Ó Caoimh, the poet, was pastor of Doneraile. An tAthair Peadar Ó Laoghaire, prolific author in the Irish language, served as a curate in the parish from 1884 to 1891. Canon Patrick A. Sheehan was parish priest from 1895 to 1913. Here he wrote most of his novels and, in capturing the spirit of the place and the time, as an author achieved extraordinary popularity and some critical acclaim.

After reading his booklet I told Caomhín about some of the historical associations of the Doneraile district. He insisted that I meet Kenneth MacGowan, his publisher, with a view to writing a booklet on Doneraile. Ken, who at that time was preparing for publication booklets of local interest under the imprint Kamac Publications, was most encouraging.

Before the end of that year he had published the first edition of *Doneraile*. Its rapid sale enabled me to bring out a revised and second edition in 1970. John B. Keane, who had spent more than a year in the town in the early 1950s as an apprentice in the pharmacy of A.H. Jones, provided a characteristically generous foreword.

Seeing how relatively straightforward it had been to prepare the first edition of *Doneraile* for publication, I asked Ken MacGowan to publish an MA thesis I had completed in UCD. He agreed to do so. *The metaphysical value and importance of the concept of being* appeared in 1969. Michael Gleeson, who helped Ken with the design and layout of his publication, provided the cover. It had a touch of genius about it: being a striking visual statement of the content of the book.

By a happy coincidence when *Doneraile* was published John J. Synon was looking around for someone to research his 'Irish roots' or even prepare an account of the Synan family for publication. In this regard he had consulted Edward MacLysaght, the distinguished genealogist. As soon as Mac, as he was generally known, read my references to the Synans in *Doneraile* he suggested to John that he enquire if I would be interested in taking up his commission.

When John met me I was flattered by his request and agreed to undertake the work, but pointed out that I had no experience of this kind of research. However, I was fortunate that at that time I had met and become a close friend of An tOllamh Pádraig de Brún of the Dublin Institute of Advanced Studies. With his invaluable help I was able to complete the project successfully.

In the event it proved to be very interesting. I was able to trace the vicissitudes of the Synans from the time their eponymous ancestor, one of the Cambro-Normans, came from Wales with Strongbow in 1172 down to the present-day Synans in Ireland and elsewhere. The family came to North Cork in the thirteenth century. Having settled, they built a number of defensive castles and forts to protect their own peculiar civil and ecclesiastical structures in the area. One of these, Castlepook, the outstanding memorial left today of the Synan family, was built by Geoffrey Synan in 1380.

John J. Synon's 'Irish roots' went back to his grandfather, Thomas. When only fourteen years old Thomas was brought to Canada in 1825 and soon afterwards to Madison, Wisconsin in the US, where he lies buried in Calvary cemetery. Thomas and his parents, James and Mary Synon, were some of those who emigrated to Canada from the north Cork district in 1824-5 when, because of serious Whiteboy disturbances, the government initiated a successful group-migration scheme from the area. In America as has happened with many other Irish surnames the spelling of the family name was altered and Synan became Synon.

John J. Synon's life-story was as interesting as that of any of his ancestors. He was born in 1909 in Virginia, where his father, Thomas Henry Synon had settled and became a landowner and a lawyer. Having attended the Blackstone Military Academy in Virginia and Stanford University in California, John worked on a number of newspapers. Following the Japanese attack on Pearl Harbour he joined the navy. After the war he married and became involved in politics in California. He ran the campaign in the southern half of the state for Goodwin Knight, the successful Republican candidate for governor. Following Knight's victory John moved to the state capital to act as one of the governor's political advisors.

Throughout that period John continued to write and contributed many pieces to the well-known Washington DC publication *Human Events*. One piece in the early 1960s, entitled 'A president from Dixie', which explained how a third-party southern candidate could challenge the Republicans and Democrats for the White House, caught the eye of Governor George Wallace of Alabama. The governor and John became friends and Wallace launched his bid for the presidency in 1968. John was one of Wallace's principal speech writers and advisors and travelled with him during the campaign. In connection with the campaign John also published *George Wallace, profile of a presidential candidate*, 200,000 copies of which were sold the summer it was issued. At that time John's weekly column of political commentary was running in 65 daily and 200 weekly newspapers. And he was much sought after in Washington for advice on political matters.

While I found researching the Synan family interesting, the most enjoyable by-product of the enterprise was the friendship of John Synon. An extraordinarily likeable person, he reminded me of Gary

Cooper, the film star. He was very tall and handsome, with the easy gestures of one who roamed the prairies and he was soft spoken with a pleasant drawl. As a journalist friend wrote in an editorial-obituary: 'John Synon had a life-long love affair with his native state of Virginia and with Ireland.' He was an unreconstructed and dedicated Southerner, devoted to all the ideals of the Old South, and we soon identified a number of issues on which we had diametrically opposed views. Not least of these was his seeming unqualified support for George Wallace who proposed some policies which had more than a whiff of racial supremacy about them.

In the early seventies John visited Ireland on quite a few occasions, mainly in his role as a journalist to view at first hand the continuing civil strife in Northern Ireland. He interviewed representatives of the main protagonists and always sought to witness disturbances or riots. On a few occasions he presented me with a rubber bullet as a souvenir of riots in Belfast or Derry.

During the course of my research he insisted that I travel to the US to meet some of his cousins in Madison, Wisconsin. While there I visited Calvary cemetery to view the family grave and headstone. Subsequently I flew into Washington DC from where John drove me to his home on Chesapeake Bay at Kilmarnock in Virginia. There followed a week's idyllic tour of important sites of the American civil war. John's greatest hero was Robert E. Lee. He became quite emotional when taking me around the huge cemetery in Richmond, where thousands of soldiers of the Confederacy lie buried. Almost as interesting as the visits to the civil war sites was meeting John's friends everywhere we over-nighted.

During the three years of my acquaintance and friendship with John he was ailing from cancer. I became aware of this when late one night I received a phone call from him. When I asked where he was he told me he was in St Vincent's Hospital, where he had been taken seriously ill a few days earlier soon after arriving in Dublin. I went in to see him. He told me that he had had 'a slow burner' for a number of years and that now after tests had been told he was fatally ill. I stayed with him until midnight. As I drove home I shed a few tears, realising how lonely it must have been for him to be in such a condition and so far as I thought from his wife, Margaret, and daughters, Molly and Mary Ellen, each of whom he idolised.

Not long after returning to the US John died. His death had for me a small added poignancy. *The Synan family*, dedicated to him and his wife, Margaret, with a foreword by Edward MacLysaght, whom he had also befriended, was not printed until some months later. I sent several copies to Margaret but sadly she did not outlive her husband for more than a year. While I never discovered what caused Margaret's death, I suspected that John's relatively young demise was due not least to the intensity with which he lived, notwithstanding his outwardly calm demeanour.

CHAPTER 3

Writers' Week

L ike other aspiring writers I have found attendance at Writers'
Week helpful in a variety of ways. It provides opportunities to
seek the advice of well-known authors and share experiences with
others who are attempting to have work published. And, apart from
the opportunity to converse with the rest of those involved in the
book trade: printers, book-designers, authors' agents, librarians, book-
reviewers and book-sellers, one meets in congenial circumstances
influential columnists and journalists.

Writers' Week was first held in 1971. Séamus Wilmot and Tim
Danaher are generally given the chief credit for its establishment. Both
were natives of Listowel and they were well placed to muster support
for a literary festival. While Séamus was registrar of the National
University of Ireland and a director of the Abbey Theatre, Tim was
attached to the radio-drama department of RTÉ.

Séamus had attended the Yeats Summer School in Sligo on a few occasions and after hearing Tim's long-playing record 'A gift of ink', which celebrated the work of writers from *Listowel and its vicinity* , suggested that a similar festival be held in his native town. They drafted a list of proposals for a festival of the arts and circulated it to members of the Kerrymen's Association in Dublin and to prominent people in Kerry. Among the latter was the secretary of Listowel Race Week Harvest Festival Committee, Nora Relihan, who at that time was thinking along the same lines. Séamus and Tim addressed an enthusiastic meeting in Listowel on the subject in November 1970. Among those present were: John B. Keane, Bryan MacMahon, Luaí Ó Murchú and Nora Relihan. A local committee was formed, with Luaí Ó Murchú as chairman, to further the project.

The first Writers' Week, from 2 to 6 June in 1971, was a success. There were lectures on the history of the area, an art exhibition, a display of books written by authors born in north Kerry and discussions on the work of George Fitzmaurice, Bryan MacMahon and John B. Keane. Plays by these local playwrights were presented each evening.

I met Séamus Wilmot early in 1971. He told me that he had read *Doneraile* and was glad I was interested in local history. However, he said: 'Fr Tony, you should focus your attention on your own area. There are very few places in the country as fascinating as North Kerry'. Then he told me about the Writers' Week to be held that summer and that the organising committee were planning to provide some lectures on the area's history and culture. He invited me to provide a talk and I replied that I would be delighted to do so. This prompted me to read all I could about the district and this proved to be but the first step in publishing a history of north Kerry.

In due course I lectured on 'Listowel and its vicinity' at the first Writers' Week. From the outset I told the organising committee to call on me if I could be helpful in any capacity. Over the years, I have given numerous talks on the history of the area, mainly in connection with the 'Historical Tour' which has been a feature of most Writers' Weeks. I also had four of my books launched in Listowel as well as launching the works of other authors. From 1983 to 1990 I had the privilege of serving as president of the festival and since then as one of its vice-presidents. And, when requested, I have over many years been pleased to be one of the sponsors of the festival.

After the first Writers' Week the organising committee decided to broaden its scope with merely special reference to the work of north Kerry authors, and to have as its main aim the encouragement of new writers. Literary competitions were organised in various categories: short story, humorous essay, poetry, one-act play, and a few years later competitions in graphic art and sculpture. These and other competitions became a permanent feature of the festival. After the first few years the announcement of the names of the winners and the presentation of prizes was transferred from the final to the opening night and followed the key-note address which preceded the formal opening of the festival. An expanded Lá na nÓg (a special programme for schoolchildren), an elaborate book fair, a number of symposia of particular interest to aspiring authors and book launchings were also added to the general format.

After the first few years the subject of the lectures was generally determined by those invited to deliver them. Down through the years a number of well-known academics, historians and *literateurs* have been heard on more than one occasion at Writers' Week. Among those were Anthony Cronin, writer and critic, Ryle Dwyer, historian, Séamus Heaney, referred to as 'The Ulster poet', Declan Kiberd, academic and author, Robert Hogan, American academic and historian, J.J. Lee, academic and historian, Hugh Leonard, playwright, John A. Murphy, academic and historian, Fintan O'Toole, journalist and author, and Reggie Smith, academic and broadcaster. Ben Kiely was the most frequent and, indeed, most popular visitor. Ben was accessible and gregarious. I was always convinced that he spoke *ex tempore*. Year after year he tended to repeat a number of favourite phrases. One of these was: 'One should never ruin a good story by telling the truth'. Each year there were at least four lectures. In 1992 there were nine, only one of which had any local reference: one which I delivered entitled' Alfred O'Rahilly, Listowel man *extraordinaire*'.

By and large the lectures were of a high standard and some were memorable. However, I also remember two for the wrong reasons. The first was at the 1972 Writers' Week. The main festival lecture was to honour Maurice Walsh and Ben Kiely was to give it. It was to be in front of O'Sullivan's public-house in Lisselton, which had been the home of Maurice Walsh. As a preliminary there was a 'location drama' on the Castle Green in Ballybunion presenting a chapter of Walsh's *The Quiet Man*. Then as the crowd gathered for the lecture Ben had to be summoned from Nolan's public-house nearby. In full view of the crowd he was helped out of a car and placed in front of the microphone. He could just about stand and in bright sunshine blinked unseeingly for five minutes before being spirited away. Desmond Fitz-Gerald, the knight of Glin, with whom I had spent the day, was sitting beside me on the high ditch. Impatient at all times, he was furious. I was very annoyed, feeling that Séamus Wilmot, Ben's friend, who had invited him to lecture, had been badly let down.

Years later I happened on an account of this incident in Gus Smith and Des Hickey's *John B: the real Keane* (Cork 1992). It read: 'Benedict Kiely, the novelist, caused a traffic jam when lecturing on Maurice Walsh outside a pub on the road to Ballybunion' I chuckled, suspecting that tongue-in-cheek this is what John B. had told the gullible authors.

The other lecture I recall was by Ulick O'Connor. He was attempting to explain the intricacies of the Noh play, a Japanese *genre* of dramatic writing. A difficult topic for anyone, the more so for a young mother who had a child with her and was trying to listen. As the child became more and more restless Ulick indicated that he could not continue unless the mother and her child left the hall. About fifteen minutes later a second such incident occurred. Ulick seemed to be oblivious of the extent to which his audience were squirming with embarrassment as the two young mothers had to leave. After the lecture a local wag who always enjoyed giving me his assessment of visitors described Ulick as 'a study in irritability'. At a previous Writers' Week he had described Hugh Leonard as 'a study in arrogance'. This last referred to behaviour in the Listowel Arms Hotel by the distinguished playwright which made it difficult for the organising committee to invite him back to the festival.

At the heart of Writers' Week are the workshops. These deal with the various categories of writing. They are directed by well-known practitioners in the short-story, poetry, the novel, biography, in writing one- or three-act plays or in preparing scripts for radio and television. One requisite for admission to a workshop is the preparation of an appropriate piece which the participant can refine during the week with the assistance of the director and the other members of the workshop.

Bryan MacMahon inaugurated this component of Writers' Week and conducted a workshop on the short story during the first year of the festival. He had seen at first hand the organisation of such workshops in the US, not least in 1965 when he had been a visiting lecturer at one of the best-known of these, that at the State University of Iowa.

It was, however, by virtue of his stature as a well-known personality that Bryan made a major contribution to the continuing success of Writers' Week. By the early 1970s he had published two collections of short stories, two books for children, two novels and three full-length plays. More importantly he had been a frequent lecturer at cultural and literary events throughout the country. In addition he was occasionally featured in programmes on Radio Éireann. Thus he was ideally suited to greet and welcome visitors to Writers' Week, a role he enjoyed immensely.

A man of great personal charm, Bryan was very popular with his fellow-townspeople and was important in ensuring local support for the festival. Like many others in Listowel, besides admiring Bryan, I had considerable affection for him. Born in 1909, after his education at the local national school, St Michael's College and St Patrick's Teacher Training College, in Drumcondra, Dublin, until he retired, he spent his life teaching third class in his native town's national school. His most endearing quality was his capacity as 'an encourager', to quote a term he liked to use. This quality he exercised to great effect both in the classroom and outside it.

Bryan had, of course, his complexities. While he had an exemplary love for his country, its culture and language, he was a quintessential romantic nationalist and would have been an easy target for revision-ist historians. Whenever a worthwhile civic initiative was taken by res-idents of the town Bryan would be to the fore urging it on. However he seldom re-appeared after the inaugural meeting. He was also exceedingly coy about letting others know how he stood on impor-tant issues. I recall on more than one occasion replies beside which the verdicts of the oracle of Delphi seemed like the essence of clarity.

Bryan was a consummate publicist. He had few equals in drawing attention to his own work. In that regard he was also an invaluable ambassador for Writers' Week and his home town. I recall on one occasion worrying out loud to Bryan about getting adequate public-ity for a book just out. 'Fr Tony', he said, 'when you have something to sell, don't shout about it down a well'.

Bryan liked to be referred to as the master. He was certainly the master of over-statement. When recalling historical events he tended – to use a favourite phrase of his – 'to gild the lily'. Such was the extent to which this was integral to his writing that I always was more impressed by Bryan in the flesh than on the page. He had few equals when it came to producing what has become known as 'the sound bite'. After once listening to a short address by him, replete with his favourite well-honed phrases, one could never forget that larger than life personality.

I never had any doubt as to who should receive most credit for the success of Writers' Week during its first thirty years. John B. Keane was so committed to it that he practically made it his own. By 1971 John B. had published twelve plays and had established himself as a play-wright of distinction. Through his self-portrait, *Letters of a successful TD*, and frequent contributions to the *Evening Herald*, *Irish Independent* and *Limerick Leader* his wit and wry humour was widely appreciated. Although basically shy, he enjoyed the company of other writers and playwrights and was able to persuade many of them to take part in Writers' Week.

Most importantly, John B. was something of a celebrity. At amateur drama festivals he had publicly protested to adjudicators whom he considered had not expressed a fair assessment of the quality of his plays. He also tended to harbour resentment against journalists and critics who wrote negative reviews of his work and on occasion verbally attacked them in public. His complaints of shabby treatment from the Abbey Theatre were intemperate. There were well-publicised clashes which arose from his association with the Language Freedom Movement, an organisation established to oppose 'compulsory Irish'. Although he loved the vernacular, John B. was irked by the compulsion employed to ensure its knowledge and use. Given his intellectual honesty and volatility, it was no surprise that when he joined the organisation he was a pro-active rather than an active member.

John B. acquired the reputation of being 'controversial' from reports of his involvement in these acrimonious incidents. This served to make him a prized guest or participant on radio and television programmes. On these programmes and in press interviews he exhibited one of his endearing qualities: his lack of equivocation. Whether they were popular or not he was always forthright in expressing his views. No mean publicist, on such occasions he exhibited as much craft in drawing attention to his work, Writers' Week and his native town as went into any of his plays.

In 1997 Listowel Urban District Council held a special meeting and civic reception in conjunction with Writers' Week. The purpose of the meeting was to confer 'the freedom of the town' on two distinguished citizens, John B. Keane and Bryan McMahon, for services rendered to literature and their town. I felt very honoured on being requested by the Writers' Week committee to present each of them to the Council on that occasion.

Two local poets contributed significantly to the success of Writers' Week. Brendan Kennelly, Ballylongford born and Trinity College academic, has conducted a number of poetry workshops and, like Bryan MacMahon and John B. Keane, acted as a literary advisor to the festival. Gabriel Fitzmaurice, Moyvane native and school principal, has been a key member of the organising committee and has contributed to numerous symposia and poetry readings.

The organising committee was fortunate in having three drama groups for presenting plays during the festival. Listowel Drama Group was founded in 1944 and, beside nurturing some remarkable local actresses, actors and producers, greatly facilitated the staging of plays by George Fitzmaurice, Bryan MacMahon and John B. Keane. In 1959 as a result of a rift between its members some resigned and established the Listowel Little Theatre Society, later re-named the Listowel Players. Subsequently John B. Keane disavowed any responsibility for the rift. However, one of the main sources of contention was a decision by the Listowel Drama Group to put on a new play by Bryan MacMahon rather than a John B. Keane play.

In 1972 a new drama group was established in happier circumstances. The multi-talented Danny Hannon re-furbished a stable and fitted it out as a fifty-seat theatre ideally suited for experimental work and intimate drama. He named it the Lartigue Little Theatre and he and the others who acted in it became known as the Lartigue Little Theatre Company. A feature of this theatre was the circular staircase by which actors descended on to the stage.

Among those at my lecture on 'Listowel and its vicinity' at the first Writers' Week was Captain Seán Feehan. Seán was the founder and proprietor of Mercier Press. He published all John B. Keane's writing. Until he died he never missed a Writers' Week.

I told Seán I was looking around for someone to publish a local history on north Kerry. He agreed to undertake this and added: 'We can sell it on the back of John B, Bryan and Writers' Week'. When I informed him about a year later that the material I had gathered and shaped would extend to over 600 printed pages he told me that the publication of a book of that size would not be a viable commercial proposition for him. I decided to publish it myself. Seán had already indicated his intention to issue it, so for 60 free copies he allowed me to leave his imprint on the proposed book.

Shane O'Neill Sinnott, proprietor of the People Newspapers Ltd., Wexford, had printed my three previous books. When I requested him to print *Listowel and its vicinity* he told me he was on the point of selling the business and suggested I contact William Britton, managing director of The Leinster Leader Ltd in Naas. Bill Britton agreed to print my book. In between issuing the weekly *Leinster Leader* the firm took in 'job-work': periodicals, the occasional book, race-cards, etc. to keep their printers busy. For me the arrangement with the firm was most accommodating. According as I had chapters ready the *Leinster Leader* set them.

In the late autumn of 1973 the book was printed. The next challenge was to sell 1,000 copies. I was aware that a book had to be promoted at two levels. One had to communicate its merits to book-sellers and librarians. This was achieved by having it reviewed in the press. But more importantly the general public had to be made aware of it. This was achieved by publicity surrounding its launch, through references to it by newspaper columnists and appearances by the author on radio and/or TV programmes.

At that time the *Late, Late Show* had few if any equals as a promotional outlet. I had little difficulty in persuading Gay Byrne's assistants to include a discussion of my book in one of the forthcoming programmes. I guaranteed to bring with me John B. Keane and Bryan MacMahon. In the event, John B. had to cry off at the last minute and was replaced by Dick Pierse. A local vet of many talents, including the gift of water-divining, Dick had a pronounced Kerry accent and, with this and his dogmatic and incisive remarks, was an excellent panellist.

As we waited in the hospitality room before going on the show I was surprised at how nervous Bryan MacMahon appeared to be. At one stage he turned to me and said: 'Fr Tony, when we go on whatever you do, don't correct me or contradict me'. Gay Byrne chatted with us about the book and asked us to remain on for the second half of the show. After the commercial break he invited on Hugh MacDiarmaid, a Scottish poet, who was also promoting a book. MacDiarmaid was a well-known Marxist and at Gay's prompting launched into a eulogy of the social system in the Soviet Union. After Bryan's injunction in the hospitality room I had spoken in the first half of the programme only when invited to do so. However, I was determined not to allow MacDiarmaid a free run on his promotion of the Communist creed. A year earlier I had spent three weeks visiting Moscow, Leningrad, Sochi on the Black Sea and Tbilisi in Georgia and had been appalled at the manner in which entire populations were enslaved under the Soviet system. Accordingly, I responded very pointedly to MacDiarmaid and illustrated my remarks by personal experiences of the 'Utopia' he lauded.

During the programme Gay Byrne held up my book for all tuned in to see it. Such was the influence of the programme that in less than six weeks all 1,000 copies had been sold! For me participation in the programme had been a revelation. I had had a very negative view of the *Late, Late Show*, being critical of the manner in which serious topics almost invariably were inadequately and unfairly presented and discussed. After seeing it from the inside I realised that it was essentially an entertainment programme and that serious subjects which would arouse controversy were introduced mainly to ensure the continuing interest of viewers. As a result of this realisation I hardly ever afterwards viewed a *Late, Late Show*. I found Gay Byrne charming before and during the programme. A few days after I had a note from him thanking me for taking part in the show and stating that he and his staff considered that it had been very successful.

I donated £2,000, the proceeds from the first edition, to the committee of the Welfare Home in Listowel. The committee had been set up a year earlier to run the Welfare Home, a refurbished TB hospital, which was intended for the elderly poor of the district. Bridie Leahy, a member of the committee, had told me they were in dire need of financial support and I promised to give them any profit which came from publishing my forthcoming book on Listowel! In less than a year I published 860 more copies of *Listowel and its vicinity* . Within a short time these also were sold and for the last twenty years this book, initially retailed at £6, has been selling at £400 a copy.

In 1985 Pan Books published *Noonday* by Robert Perrin. It was a splendid, immensely successful historical novel of 680 pages. The extent to which it was based on, and imaginatively enhanced, the narrative of *Listowel and its vicinity* was remarkable. After I had communicated with the publishers I received due acknowledgement and compensation.

The preparation of *Listowel and its vicinity* for publication initiated three life-long friendships with persons who took a keen and immensely helpful interest in this and all my subsequent writings. I first met Helen Murray as a parishioner in St Joseph's, Eastwall. She was employed in the accounts department of Grant Barnett & Co and later became manager of the Eastwall Credit Union. She agreed to type whatever material I drafted each week. In so doing she eventually prepared the typescripts of ten of my books for publication.

Dr Pádraig de Brún, born in Listowel but raised in Lixnaw and Ballyduff, was a member of the Dublin Institute for Advanced Studies from 1966 to 1998. A renowned scholar with a prodigious output, his knowledge of the local history of his county is unrivalled. His insistence on accuracy and fairness has left its mark on most of my work.

Maurice O'Connell, native of Moyvane, distinguished civil servant, governor of the Central Bank from 1994 to 2002 and member of the board of the European Central Bank from 1999 to 2002 is another life-long friend who has contributed much that is valuable in my publications. No matter what the calls on his time he has always read and judiciously improved anything I have prepared for publication.

When I consider these friendships I realise that I am indebted more than most to Writers' Week and its prompting me to publish *Listowel and its vicinity* .

CHAPTER 4

Interviews

One of the great pleasures in preparing a book for publication is the opportunity to seek out and engage interesting and distinguished persons. In this regard over the years I have interviewed hundreds of persons. With just one exception all agreed to meet me. When I requested an interview from Seán Ó Faoláin he suggested we talk on the telephone, as he was unwell.

At the time I was collecting material on Alfred O'Rahilly in his role as an academic. He had helped Ó Faoláin to win a travelling fellowship to do post-graduate work in the US under the Commonwealth (Harkness) Fund. By a curious coincidence, while Ó Faoláin was availing of this scholarship in Harvard in 1926-7, O'Rahilly was also there on a sabbatical. In his autobiography *Vive Moi* Ó Faoláin refers to this and the fact that later O'Rahilly supported him in his unsuccessful application for the chair of English in UCC. I was disappointed to discover that the distinguished writer could not add much more than was contained in his autobiography, as the two had scarcely ever met while at Harvard or thereafter.

I was conscious that as a priest I had a definite advantage when requesting and conducting interviews. This was very much the case with the discussion of a person's involvement in embarrassing or controversial events. I also set out to win the confidence of interviewees. Many persons were uncomfortable at the prospect of an interview being put on a tape-recorder so I seldom used one. I also guaranteed that I would place before them what I had written from the information they gave me and would not print it unless they had been satisfied with its accuracy and balance.

With a few exceptions I was favourably impressed by those I interviewed. One such exception was Peadar O'Donnell. I had a long and enjoyable exchange with Peadar. With justification he was held in high regard in trade-union, Labour, Republican and literary circles. He exhibited extraordinary friendliness towards me, recalled his friendship with a number of priests and I was aware that he was at the time a practising Catholic. Yet at the same time he was revelling in his public reputation of being an anti-clerical and an agnostic. I disliked that phoney dichotomy and was sorely tempted to tell him so.

I interviewed Tod Andrews in connection with the final months of the civil war. He had been adjutant to Liam Lynch, OC of the anti-treaty forces. With other leaders, including Austin Stack, he was in the area, where Lynch was fatally wounded in April 1923. He was helpful, though in a pronounced self-serving way, in recalling what those leaders were saying and doing until the civil war petered out in May. Unlike Peadar O'Donnell, he was devoid of charm. Nor was I impressed at the entirely negative assessment he gave of his former colleagues or indeed any person mentioned during the interview.

A number of interviews remain fixed in my mind for other reasons. In 1976, after reading *Memoirs of Constable Jeremiah Mee, RIC*, Mrs Nanette Barrett requested me to write a biography of her uncle, Austin Stack. She told me she had a number of letters by and to Stack which had until then not been seen outside the family circle. Dan Nolan of Anvil Books in Tralee was enthusiastic at the prospect of publishing such a book.

When I delivered the typescript to Dan he told me it would run to more than 400 printed pages, and, consequently, would not be a financial success. He gave me two options. I could reduce the material to produce a book of about 200 pages, preferably 192, a multiple of 32, or, if I gave him £1,000, he would publish the typescript as it was. I consulted my friend, Seán Ó Lúing, who had been most helpful in my research. When I told him of my dilemma he advised: 'Fr Tony, publish everything'. This I did and in the event the book realised not a loss but a profit of £2,000!

Before beginning work on Austin Stack I told Nanette Barrett that there were episodes in her uncle's life in which he seemed to be less than heroic. I instanced his walking into the RIC barracks in Tralee during Easter week 1916 and the circumstances surrounding his capture towards the end of the civil war in 1923. Every biographer, I pointed out, like everyone else, tended to view the world and issues from where he or she stood. But, while I would view Austin Stack from an Irish nationalist perspective, the basic imperative for the biographer was to collect as much information and evidence as possible and to follow the evidence wherever it led. Nanette indicated that she would be happy with a 'warts and all' biography.

I was surprised by what my research disclosed. Austin Stack indicated in private and occasionally in public his pride in his father, William Moore Stack, generally regarded as a Fenian hero and martyr. However, the difference between the idealised version of William Moore Stack, the Fenian, and the reality was considerable. Some months after being imprisoned at the end of 1866 for his Fenian activities he produced an extraordinary document in which he conveyed to the authorities every item of information which he could recall about the Fenian organisation, its leadership and members. He also wrote requesting 'that some experienced person should be instructed to see me when it is probable that many things which do not occur to me may be elicited on a personal interview'. In this same statement he made the revealing remark that he was for some time about the turn of 1865-6 suspected by his comrades of giving information to the government. The authorities, it seems, were already aware of this and of Moore Stack's standing among some of his Fenian comrades, how they regarded him as a man in whom no trust could be placed, as he was credulous, very fond of drink and 'spoke rather freely'.

There were also questionable incidents in Austin Stack's own life. He was OC of the Irish Volunteers in Tralee who were charged with the supervision of the planned arms landing at Fenit in 1916. Yet in the midst of the confusion after Sir Roger Casement and his companions landed on Banna Strand he walked into the RIC barracks in Tralee, with incriminating evidence on his person and knowing that he would be detained. Then there was Stack's capture towards the end of the civil war which had all the appearance of his handing himself up unarmed to Irish Free State troops at a time when colleagues were being executed after capture in possession of arms.

Mrs Nanette Barrett was pleased with the appearance of *Austin Stack: portrait of a separatist*. But she had serious reservations about these and a number of other items in the book. In a difficult interview she told me so in no uncertain manner. I was at pains to point out that her uncle like every other human being was not flawless but that, notwithstanding this, no one could doubt Austin Stack's commitment and dedication to whatever task he had on hand or his major and unique contribution to the struggle for independence.

Another interview which I had reason to vividly recall was in connection with *The Knights of Glin*. I first met Desmond John Villiers Fitz-Gerald, the present knight of Glin, at Writers' Week in 1971. A person of considerable charm, he was an enthusiastic supporter of the festival from its inception, served as its president in 1978 and 1979 and since then has been one of its vice-presidents. I always enjoy renewing his acquaintance as we meet each year in Listowel.

Born in 1937, after his early education in Canada he eventually graduated from Harvard. He specialised in the study of Irish architecture and the Irish decorative arts and from 1965 to 1975 was an assistant (and later deputy-keeper) in the department of furniture and woodwork in the Victoria and Albert Museum, London. From 1978 onwards he has been representative in Ireland for Christie's, the London-based fine art auctioneers, and has taken a more direct part in the running of his estate. He has also opened Glin Castle to the public and established a restaurant and tourist shop on his demesne.

Desmond is proud of his ancient family, particularly so of his Anglo-Norman forebears and the manner in which in centuries past they became more Irish than the Irish themselves. I have been occasionally surprised at his lack of empathy for fellow Irish Protestants who are of Elizabethan, Cromwellian or Williamite extraction.

In 1977 he commissioned me to prepare a history of the knights of Glin. A great deal of material was available on the knights and the district of Glin, especially in the eighteenth and nineteenth centuries, owing to the research of local historian, Thomas F. (Mac) Culhane. Desmond also was most helpful, having done considerable research into the history of his family. From time to time he would telephone me with new information or send me notes on items he had checked out in London. However, so indecipherable was his writing that sometimes I would have to ring him up to learn what he had written!

A number of the knights of Glin were eccentric. Of these John Fraunceis Fitz-Gerald (1791-1854) was the most colourful. His weakness for the fair-sex was a by-word, as was indicated by the nickname given him by the local people – ridire na mBan (the knight of the women). Local tradition recorded that mainly on that account he had numerous clashes with the parish priest of Glin at that time, the equally formidable Fr Daniel O'Sullivan.

I was given access to the Estate Rental by the knight and to the parish records by Fr Gerald Griffin, then parish priest of Glin. With these I made some interesting discoveries, one of which was that John Fraunceis had fathered a son with an illegitimate daughter. I informed Desmond of this and that I would mention this in the text only if he was happy that it be included.

Desmond purported to be an archetypal liberal, especially in the area of sexual morality. On a few occasions friends of his told me jokingly that when he had been at Harvard he was known not as the knight of Glin but as the night of sin! His first reaction to my surprise at the discovery and my query as to how we should deal it was: 'Tony, don't be such a Puritan'. In any case he said he would consult his friends in the artistic and literary fraternities in Dublin on the matter and let me have a decision. In less than a week he replied that the unanimous advice he had received was to publish everything, including the incident involving incest.

Six weeks later he drove up from Glin to tell me that after he had informed the family about the item they were adamant that it should not be published. This was not the last word on the matter. During Writers' Week 1978 he told me that his mother wished that I join her for tea some afternoon. A formidable lady, Veronica Villiers was the granddaughter of Lord Wimbourne, a former lord lieutenant of Ireland, and first cousin of Sir Winston Churchill. In 1929 she married the then knight of Glin. After her husband died in 1949 she was left in severely straitened circumstances. But she managed to avoid selling Glin Castle and estate. In 1954 she married Canadian and widower Horatio Ray Milner, an oil man, president of a natural gas company and a millionaire. The marriage rescued the family from insolvency. After her second husband died in 1975 she was left a very wealthy person and her word held sway in the extended Glin family.

On my arrival for afternoon tea I was led to the lawn at the front of the castle. It was a glorious day and Madam Fitz-Gerald was waiting for me. She was a person of generous proportions. In this regard I was reminded of Winston Churchill. The hat she wore was like a small umbrella. As we sat alone at the table which appeared to me to be like the display counter of a confectioner's shop we were attended by a formally-attired butler. She asked me what kind of tea I would have. Apparently there were three kinds on offer! She asked me what I would have in it. Again there were a number of options. As I looked round there was no milk in sight but I had not the courage to send the butler to the kitchen for some and opted for lemon. After exchanging a few pleasantries Madam Fitz-Gerald was most engaging. She recalled her life at Glin Castle, especially the difficult times during the war years. Then after her husband died and left her a heavily mortgaged estate she had an anxious time, with the responsibility of running a farm and raising three children. It was by selling produce from her kitchen garden to the catering centre at Foynes, then terminus of the transatlantic flying-boats, that she was able to send the present knight to preparatory school. Eventually she got round to telling me at some length what little regard she had for authors who delighted in highlighting the scandals and 'skeletons' of well-known families.

In the event I did not include a reference to the instance of incest. But I was amused at the irony whereby those of us who purport to be liberal in our outlook tend to re-focus our attitudes when an issue affects ourselves. Years later I was amused at another irony. On the two occasions I dined in Glin Castle, Olda, Desmond's wife, was at pains to tell me that what we were served were her own recipes. She was of Dutch extraction and said they were representative of Dutch cuisine. I found the meals quite strange and not to my liking. Many years later I met Desmond. He was promoting a book on recipes to which Olda had contributed!

One of the most enjoyable and interesting interviews I ever had was with Lord Listowel. When I was researching *Listowel and its vicinity* I wrote to him and indicated that I intended to include a chapter on the Anglo-Irish families associated with North Kerry, of which his was the principal one. I enquired if he had any family papers which I could consult and requested an interview to discuss the matter. He replied that he was not aware of any family papers other than those lodged in official archives. With regard to an interview he suggested that when I had completed my draft on his family I send it to him and subsequently we could have a useful meeting about it.

In due course after he had seen the draft he arranged to meet me in the palace of Westminster. I looked forward to the meeting with eager anticipation. The Right Honourable William Francis Hare was born in 1906 and was the family's most distinguished and talented member to date. After schooling at Eton he went to Oxford and later Cambridge where, becoming a convinced socialist, he joined the Labour Party and announced that, disapproving of titles, he wished in future to be known as Mr Hare. A formidable philosopher, he published *The values of life* in 1931 and *A critical history of modern aesthetics* in 1933. In 1937 after service in the army he entered public life as a county councillor for London. From 1965 to 1976 he was lord chairman of committees and deputy speaker of the House of Lords. Earlier he was postmaster general and secretary of state for India from 1945 to 1947, governor general and commander in chief of Ghana from 1957 to 1960, and a member of the privy council of Great Britain.

When I arrived at the houses of parliament I was led to his imposing office on the second floor. We chatted informally for some time and I was surprised at how much he already knew about me. He told me his wife, the former Pamela Reid, had read my chapter on the family and was as pleased with it as he was and that she was coming up to London to have lunch with us.

After lunch we had a most productive and helpful session on the draft. However it was clear that he was far more interested in philosophy than history. At the time he was rated in academic circles with Bertrand Russell, the philosopher, and A.J. Ayer, the logical positivist. He presented me with a signed copy of *Modern aesthetics: an historical introduction*. This was a revised edition of his earlier work on the subject and was published in 1967. He gave me an enthralling summary of its content.

Then he asked me if I would like to see the palace. I told him it was something I had been looking forward to. As we descended the wide staircase from his office we met Lord O'Neill of the Maine, the former Captain Terence O'Neill. He had resigned the leadership of the Unionist Party in 1969, from politics in 1970 and had just published his autobiography in 1972. Both lords greeted each other very warmly. Listowel introduced me to Lord O'Neill and told him about the purpose of my visit to Westminster. O'Neill was exceptionally friendly and the three of us spent five minutes chatting about the challenges and pitfalls of publishing. I was surprised at how imposing a figure O'Neill was. He stood well over six feet.

Further down the stairs we met Lord George-Brown, a former deputy leader of the Labour Party. It seems he alternated between two moods: he could be either ebullient or angry and morose. At that time he was in a most ebullient mood. When Listowel told him about the proposed book on North Kerry, George-Brown told me he was a

Corkman and proud to be so. He had a high-pitched voice and I was surprised at how large and tall he was. Listowel introduced me to a number of other MPs. I was struck by the congenial and friendly atmosphere of the place. The people we met were totally relaxed and seemed to be simply sauntering about. I was reminded of the oft-repeated remark that the palace of Westminster was the best club in the world. Eventually we arrived at the terrace of the House of Lords, beside the Thames. Groups of people were having afternoon tea. Listowel led me to one group and introduced me to Mrs Pandit Nehru, a former Indian high commissioner in London and sister of Jawaharlal Nehru, the Indian statesman.

When he left me to the door Listowel invited me to lunch again with him when I was next in London. This invitation I availed of about six weeks after the publication of *Listowel and its vicinity* . In the meantime I had sent him copies of the book and he had expressed his satisfaction with the final version of the chapter on his family. On the second occasion I had lunch with him he told me he had presented a copy of the book to the library of the palace of Westminster and that the librarian had had it beautifully bound. He scribbled a note and sent for the book. It arrived before we had finished lunch. As I looked at the book I realised that no new binding had been attached to it. It was bound in the same way as every other copy. The dust-cover had simply been removed. I did not disclose this to Listowel but soon after returning home I was delighted to be able to inform Tommy Duffy, book-binder to the *Leinster Leader*, of the high regard in which his book-binding skill was held in London!

Another interview with a representative of an Anglo-Irish family associated with the Listowel district led to a life-time friendship. The knights of Kerry belong to an early branch of the mighty Geraldines. Although not as prominent in Irish history as the houses of Kildare or Desmond, nonetheless from the thirteenth century onwards they played a significant role in ecclesiastical and civil affairs. Until the second half of the seventeenth century they held large estates in five of the eight baronies of county Kerry. Then over the next hundred years, owing mainly to the vicissitudes of history, they lost practically all their estates. At the beginning of the nineteenth century all that was left to the family was an estate on Valentia Island and another in the vicinity of Listowel.

Ballinruddery: Baile an Ridire (the town of the knight), the name of the strip of land along the southern bank of the Feale, near Listowel, recalls the association of the knights of Kerry with this district. In this area also stands the ruins of a FitzGerald castle. Almost certainly it was reduced by Sir Charles Wilmot in 1602 during the Elizabethan conquest. The knights of Kerry returned to reside here about eighty years later at Ballinruddery House, described as a beautiful thatched mansion. After this was burnt accidentally in the second half of the nineteenth century the family resided for the most part on their Valentia estate. In the twentieth century members of the family, not least Arthur Henry Brinsley FitzGerald, the 22nd knight, kept up their association with Ireland.

When I had completed a draft on the knights of Kerry I sent it to Adrian FitzGerald, son of the 23rd knight of Kerry, with a request for help to improve it. A mutual friend had told me that he was particularly interested in his family background and Irish heritage. Adrian contacted me and said he would be spending a weekend at his small summer house on Valentia Island with his sister and her young daughter during the following week, and invited me to join them. My visit was both enjoyable and very useful. The imposing residence at Glanleam, built by Maurice FitzGerald, 18th knight of Kerry, in 1820, was occupied by Colonel and Mrs Richard J. Uniacke. During my stay with Adrian I was invited to a lunch at Glanleam attended by the surviving gentry of Co Kerry. Two recollections of it survive. On leaving the dining-room the men and women adjourned to separate rooms, and earlier during a discussion on education I learned that those who had school-going children had sent them to be educated in England.

Since that visit to Valentia Island Adrian and I have been friends. An archetypal English gentleman, he is proud of his Irish heritage and, apart from being a supporter of the Wexford Opera Festival, a frequent visitor to the country. Civic-minded rather than ambitious, he has been active in Conservative Party politics, has served as a member of Kensington and Chelsea Borough Council since 1974, was mayor in 1984-5 and chairman of its Education Committee 1995-98. He was chairman of the Anglo-Polish Society in 1989-92, is vice-president of the London branch of the Irish Georgian Society, president of the Benevolent Society of St Patrick and a member of the council of the Irish Association of the Order of Malta. In 2001 on the death of his father he became 6th baronet and 24th knight of Kerry. A few years earlier he had 'read' himself into the Catholic Church. This came as no surprise to me. An avid and reflective reader and committed member of the Church of England, whenever he stayed with me over a weekend he was eager to attend Sunday Mass and when the opportunity arose opted for one in the Irish language!

Judge Dermot Kinlen was one of the most colourful persons I interviewed in connection with the publication of a book. In 1978 he set up a trust, the purpose of which was to commission a biography of his grandfather, Judge Thomas O'Donnell. The members of the trust were: Mrs Kathleen Browne, Kerry County Librarian; Walter McGrath, sub-editor *Cork Examiner*; and Canon John McKenna, P.P., Castletownbere: all friends of mine. So when they asked me to take on the commission I was very pleased to accede to their request.

Thomas O'Donnell was born at Liscarney, near Dingle, in 1871. After qualifying at Marlborough Street Training College he taught in Killorglin national school from 1892 to 1900. Then from 1900 to 1918 he was MP for West Kerry. In 1926 with Captain William A. Redmond, TD, he co-founded the Irish National League. He was a forceful advocate of the coalition of the Irish National League, Labour and Fianna Fáil Parties which narrowly failed to replace the Cumann na nGaedheal government in 1927. With the formal dissolution of the Irish National League in 1931 he joined Fianna Fáil. In 1932 he was called to the inner bar, in 1938 was appointed chairman of the Military Pensions' Board and in 1941 became judge in the Clare, Kerry and Limerick circuit courts. He died two years later.

O'Donnell, son of an evicted tenant farmer, had little difficulty in identifying with the interests of his constituents and was ever their effective advocate. Forthright and mercurial, he was driven by single-minded ambition. He radically changed his loyalties according to changing circumstances and was occasionally the centre of bitter controversy.

During the preparation of the book I frequently met Dermot Kinlen and discovered that he was as distinguished as his grandfather. After a brilliant academic course he rose steadily through the ranks of the legal profession: senior counsel of the Irish bar 1971, deputy judge to the court of appeal O.E.C.D. Paris 1990, judge to the court of appeal O.E.C.D. 1993 and judge of the Irish high court 1993. Determined to use his legal contacts and expertise in the service of others, Dermot has been active in areas beyond the strict parameters of his profession. In 1977 he visited China with the former president of Ireland, Cearbhal Ó Dálaigh, as a guest of the Chinese government and was subsequently involved in establishing diplomatic relations between both countries. A guest of the Chinese in 1980, 1983 and 1985, in 1998 he led a delegation of Irish judges to lecture the Chinese judiciary on human rights, independence of judiciary, etc. In 1980, as a result of an international request, he visited the re-education camps and prisons of Vietnam as a guest of Premier Pham Van Dong and published a report on his findings. At home he has been a member of the visiting committee of St Patrick's Institution for Juvenile Offenders from 1971 to 1996 and chairman of the visiting committee for Mountjoy prison from 1990 to 1993. After he retired from the bench in 2002 he was appointed inspector-general of prisons and places of detention.

During our collaboration on the biography of his grandfather, Dermot told me that he now regarded me as one of his close friends. Such friends receive many kindnesses from Dermot. Among those is an open invitation to one or other of his summer residences at Sneem in Co Kerry, where one can find oneself in the company of the great and the good of the land. And each Christmas he sends a round letter sharing news about projects in which he and his friends have been involved. At Sneem Dermot is at his happiest adopting an avuncular attitude to his guests and attempting to anticipate their wishes. Ever eager to enhance his adopted village, he has established there an international culture park. There are, it seems, other ways in which he makes the village attractive to tourists. Some years ago a German journalist wrote that one of the attractions of a stay in the Sneem district was 'a delightfully eccentric Irish judge who resides nearby'.

CHAPTER 5

Forewords

A few years ago a book consisting of a selection of forewords achieved considerable commercial and literary success in the UK. This was not surprising as forewords generally are contributed by persons who are exceptional writers and well-known. The aim of the foreword is to introduce the book and whet the reader's appetite by providing a short abstract of the book's content, highlighting its merits and emphasising the author's practical knowledge of the subject treated. In determining to include a foreword in *Doneraile*, my first literary effort, I was also prompted by the need to have the endorsement of an established writer.

I was fortunate in having on hand the ideal person to draft a foreword for *Doneraile*. John B. Keane had spent more than a year in the early 1950s in the village as an apprentice in the pharmacy of Arthur H. Jones, tireless collector of books, silver and furniture, and a remarkable personality in his own right. In a splendid piece John B. showed that he had absorbed the unique atmosphere of the place. With his mind focused on writing plays he concluded: 'The chapter on the Doneraile conspiracy may well inspire a dramatist to bring its macabre plot before the footlights'.

The foreword by Edward MacLysaght to *The Synan family* arose from the provenance of the book. MacLysaght was and had been for some time the leading authority on the origin and names of Irish families. Although a friend of John and Margaret Synon, when they requested him to publish a history of their family he pleaded inability, owing to pressure of work. When I agreed to attempt this he promised to help in any way I wished, which he did. As I was neither a genealogist nor had any previous experience of preparing a family history, I was glad to have his approval in the shape of a foreword.

For a foreword for *Listowel and its vicinity* I never had anyone in mind apart from Bryan MacMahon. In preparing the book for publication I consulted him frequently for advice and information. He was fulsome with both. Moreover, his encouragement and support, and his positive and upbeat appraisal of all things Irish and Kerry was contagious. The foreword he supplied is a neat example of his literary style, more a piece of rhetoric than of writing and as redolent of heart as much as head.

Listowel and its vicinity included an account of a mutiny by members of the Royal Irish Constabulary in Listowel police barracks in June 1920. Following its publication Mrs Michael Doyle contacted me. She told me she was Eileen Mee, eldest daughter of Jeremiah Mee, who had played a central role in the insubordination in Listowel barracks. Her father had been obsessed by the incident and had left voluminous accounts of that historic event. Eileen was eager that the fullest possible account of all the circumstances surrounding the incident be brought to the attention of the public.

With Eileen's help I prepared a condensed version of her father's recollections. Dan Nolan of Anvil Books agreed to publish it. All three of us, however, were acutely aware that its publication might be seen as a piece of Republican propaganda. Because of the grave situation in Northern Ireland at that time a propaganda war was being waged on the airwaves and in the press. It was essential that the proposed publication be seen as a contribution to the literature of the war of independence rather than as a tract for the times.

I asked Colonel Dave Neligan to help by providing a foreword. From the time of his involvement in the civil war in Kerry in 1922–23 he had been a 'hate-figure' for Republicans. Thus his foreword would not be seen as providing endorsement for current Republican activists. Moreover there was a striking analogy between Dave's 'national record' and that of Mee. Both had joined the police. While Mee was a constable in the RIC, Dave was a detective in the Dublin Metropolitan Police. Both had become disillusioned at the prospect of being used by the British against their own people and both, at a grave risk to their lives, made significant contributions to the struggle for independence. In his foreword Dave did exactly what was required. Subsequently I came to know him quite well. He was a most likeable person and not at all the ogre Kerry anti-treatyites had made him out to be.

After the publication of *Memoirs of Constable Jeremiah Mee, RIC* I was determined that Mee and his comrades would receive further public acknowledgement for their courageous stand. The more I reflected on the matter the more I became convinced that it had been a most significant incident in Ireland's war of independence. As news of the refusal of the fifteen constables to be transferred and to hand their barracks at Listowel to the military spread throughout the RIC and later appeared in the press, the pace of members of the force taking early retirement or being dismissed quickened. Eventually by 1 March 1921, 2,570 members had left the force. Their places were taken by the hastily-recruited Black and Tans. For the most part, these were ex-soldiers and they received little, if any, serious police training. Their indiscipline and the outrages for which they were responsible alienated the Irish people, most of whom had no enthusiasm whatsoever for the policy and actions of Sinn Féin and the IRA. The result was that the crown forces had to operate in an increasingly hostile environment which cast serious doubts on their capacity to pacify successfully the country.

I conceived the idea of erecting a plaque to honour the policemen involved in that historic event in an alcove at the main entrance to Listowel Garda Station, which was the former RIC barracks. Apart from the names of the constables and the date of the incident it would include the RIC crest and the heading 'The king's servants but Ireland's first'. At that time Tony O'Callaghan was acquiring a national reputation for producing beautifully-crafted artistic plaques in copper. I consulted Tony on the matter and he was most supportive and insisted on donating the plaque. To request the formal permission of the department of justice I formed a committee, with Frank Hanly, the local superintendent, as chairman and Mrs Eileen Doyle, John B. Keane, Mrs Susan McKenna, Bryan McMahon and myself as members. The time was not congenial for such a project. However, after much lobbying the erection of the plaque was authorised by Gerry Collins, minister for justice, and it was formally unveiled by the chairman of Listowel Urban District Council during Writers' Week in June 1978.

The publication of *Memoirs of Constable Jeremiah Mee, RIC* was generously covered in the media, as was the erection of the plaque in 1978. Then a local committee, with representatives from Glenamaddy and Williamstown, County Galway, was formed in 1987 to honour their native son. Senator Tom Hussey and Superintendent John Mee, a nephew of Jerry Mee, was also members of the committee. Eventually a memorial to Mee was erected at the crossroads in Glenamaddy on 10 September 1989. After celebrating a memorial Mass for Mee and his comrades I unveiled the memorial in the presence of members of the Mee family and a large gathering.

I continued my interest in police history, especially the early years of the Garda Síochána. With the assistance of Patrick Joseph Carroll, a former deputy commissioner, and John M. Shaw, both early members of the force, I collected the recollections and photographs of some of their colleagues who had served from the time of its establishment and during the two decades that followed. When I realised I would not have the opportunity to fulfil a promise to John Shaw to prepare a book on the first twenty-five years of the Garda Síochána I gave these to Gregory Allen who published *The Garda Síochána: policing independ-*

ent Ireland 1922-82 in 1999. From its inception in 1995 I have been a member of the Garda History Society and am now an honorary member.

One hopes that a foreword would increase interest in a book. This was certainly my main motivation in providing forewords to books by and on Alfred O'Rahilly. In 1984 Fr Michael McCarthy, CSSp, Irish provincial, and Con Murphy, rights commissioner, called on me. Both had been close friends of Alfred O'Rahilly, and had for some time been attempting unsuccessfully to have O'Rahilly's last work published. This combined detailed treatments of the passion and death of Christ, its artistic depiction throughout the centuries and the shroud of Turin. At their request I undertook to publish the book on which very little further work was needed.

As *The crucified* was a theological tract I considered that it required an endorsement by a theologian. My first choice for this was Kevin McNamara. He had spent much of his life on the theology faculty in St Patrick's College, Maynooth, and was then serving as bishop of Kerry. In both assignments he won the respect of his peers and many others besides. From the outset Kevin McNamara was most interested in the project. He told me that he was familiar with much of what O'Rahilly had written and that he had made his acquaintance when studying for a H.Dip. in Ed. at University College, Cork, in 1952-3. After reading the proofs he provided a characteristically carefully-written and judicious foreword.

To enable me to write an adequate introduction to *The crucified* I was given access to the huge cache of papers left by Alfred O'Rahilly. I was fascinated by the information therein and was easily persuaded to prepare a biography of that remarkable polymath. Eventually, mainly for commercial reasons, this was published in four volumes.

During most of his life O'Rahilly was a leading figure in the academic world. Besides, he played a major role in public affairs, was a tireless advocate of social reform and a fearless Catholic apologist. Con Murphy suggested that it would be appropriate that forewords to the volumes be written by persons eminent in these various fields. At that time there were few persons in the country who had the stature of

T. Kenneth Whitaker as a public servant and economist. In addition, after retiring from the governership of the Central Bank he had become chancellor of the National University of Ireland and chairman of Bord na Gaeilge. Whitaker, in expressing his pleasure at being invited to provide the foreword for *Alfred O'Rahilly I: Academic*, recalled that his first important assignment in the department of finance was to prepare a detailed rebuttal of the heterodox economics featured in O'Rahilly's massive tome *Money* published in Cork and London in 1941.

Alfred O'Rahilly II: Public figure was ready for publication in 1989. Apart from being Taoiseach, Charles J. Haughey was serving as president of the European Union. At that extremely busy time the Taoiseach, through the good offices of John Stafford, TD, agreed to provide a foreword for the forthcoming volume. It was drafted by his aide, the historian Martin Mansergh, and arrived in good time.

O'Rahilly was one of the dominant influences on the labour and social history of his time. This he achieved by his remarkably successful promotion of the study of Catholic sociology through extra-mural and extension courses at University College, Cork, and by his close friendship with key trade-union leaders. I was fortunate in having Anthony Coughlan write the foreword to the volume on O'Rahilly as a social reformer. Head of the department of social studies at Trinity College, Dublin, there is much of Alfred O'Rahilly in Coughlan. He courageously challenges the accepted wisdom on a range of crucial social issues and is a tireless upholder of the democratic rights of people at national and international level. When he was president of UCC, O'Rahilly personally welcomed each new undergraduate to college and gave the same advice to each of them. Coughlan told me that this advice: 'Be of good character' remained ever fresh in his memory.

O'Rahilly was a person of extraordinary versatility, equally at home in science, philosophy, economics, sociology and theology. He enjoyed disputation and was embroiled in controversies in each of these disciplines throughout his life. The press, however, gave most coverage to his interventions where questions of religion and/or morality were discussed and for a period covering two generations he was regarded as Ireland's leading Catholic apologist. In this context he was as eagerly read across the Catholic English-speaking world as Douglas Hyde and Frank Sheed in Britain or B.A. (Bob) Santamaria, the champion of Catholic Action, in Australia. For a foreword in the volume which dealt with Alfred O'Rahilly as a Catholic apologist I went back to UCC. Similar to O'Rahilly in his dedication to scholarship and his frenetic activity, historian Professor J.J. Lee in a perceptive piece acknowledged O'Rahilly's outstanding gifts and achievements and emphasised the imperative of assessing historical figures in the circumstances of their times.

Well schooled by Con Murphy on the importance of having a book 'fronted by a top person', I was fortunate in having *Olivia Mary Taaffe 1832-1918: foundress of St Joseph's Young Priests Society* introduced by Eileen Sparling. She was serving as president of the Society, which promotes vocations to the priesthood, and had responsibility for the Society's centenary celebrations. One of the main projects planned was the preparation of a biography of the foundress and I was commissioned to supply this. In her foreword Eileen recorded the Society's appreciation, and indeed that of all helped by it, to 'the many thousands of ordinary grass root members who have worked for the Society over the years'. She continued: 'Many of them have worked for long periods and in some instances for periods of in excess of fifty years'.

Martin Mansergh provided the foreword for *Memoirs of Senator Joseph Connolly*: a founder of modern Ireland. For a number of years whenever I had met him he had expressed his regret that a number of important memoirs had not been published and made generally available to historians. Among these were the memoirs of Senator Joseph Connolly, those of Mrs Kathleen Clarke and those of Senator James G. Douglas. I was particularly interested in the first of these. Through my friendship with a colleague, Fr Brian Connolly, son of Senator Connolly, I had had access to them. I was also able to ensure that a number of historians and writers, including Tim Pat Coogan, T. Ryle Dwyer, Proinsias MacAonghusa and Martin Mansergh, had an opportunity to examine them. When I approached the Connolly family with a view to preparing them for publication they were quite pleased. It seems that, owing to their voluminous nature, publishers did not consider that their publication would be a satisfactory commercial undertaking. In his foreword Martin Mansergh expressed his pleasure that the memoirs were now available to historians.

The immensely popular Dr Tom Murphy, who was president of UCD from 1972 to 1985, agreed to provide a foreword to *Newman's University Church: a history and a guide*. However, he died before doing so and in his place Art Cosgrove, the serving president, supplied an appropriate envoi for it.

After the memoirs of Senator Joseph Connolly appeared, William Corbett, of Drombane, Thurles, Co Tipperary, a keen student of Irish history, wrote suggesting that I publish those of Senator James G. Douglas. This prompted me to call on the family when I discovered that, in addition to the typescript of the memoirs, they had a large collection of his papers. They were pleased when I offered with the help of these to publish an annotated version of the Douglas memoirs. As the book would be of fairly limited interest I was grateful when University College Dublin Press of my *alma mater* took responsibility for its publication. I was even more gratified when Brian Farrell provided the foreword. A fellow-student in the history department of UCD, we had kept in touch through the years. Brian developed a passion for the study of democratic politics and spent most of his life lecturing on the subject in UCD and as a leading broadcaster on that topic in RTÉ.

In another context a complaint was made that the best wine was kept until last. I felt this was the case with regard to the foreword in *At the coalface: recollections of a city and country priest 1950-2000*. In an excellent foreword Cardinal Cahal B. Daly captured the spirit and substance of the book.

CHAPTER 6

Publicity

For a book to sell people must be aware of it, hence the importance of publicity. Well known writers have little difficulty in generating publicity for forthcoming books. That is not accessible to most other writers. My experience of the one occasion when I succeeded in generating considerable pre-publication publicity caused me subsequently to be cautious about such an exercise.

The book in question was *Thomas Johnson 1872-1963: first leader of the Labour Party in Dáil Éireann* (Dublin 1980). Work on this biography was begun by Seán MacCormac who in 1973-4 had numerous interviews with Mrs Marie Johnson. She also gave him her papers and those of her husband which had not already been deposited in the National Library of Ireland. By 1977 Seán had produced preliminary drafts of the first few chapters. From early 1975 onwards he met me once a month to discuss the progress of his work. After a brief illness he died on 17 June 1977. That autumn at a special meeting of the Blackrock Literary and Debating Society, of which Seán had been vice-president, I had the honour of paying a tribute to my late friend. Subsequently his widow, Nuala, suggested that I complete the biography and to that end placed at my disposal the Johnson papers Seán had had in his possession.

I met John Feeney at Writers' Week, Listowel, in June 1979. He was covering the festival for the *Sunday Independent*. John asked me what book I was working on. When I told him I was preparing a biography of Tom Johnson, co-founder and first leader of the Labour Party, he was immediately interested. He was even more so when I told him that the more I researched the period the greater the gap I was discovering between the real James Larkin and the then-current myth which had been developed around him.

John suggested that I give him an interview on the proposed book, especially with regard to my perspective on Larkin. I agreed to do so when I had completed my research. We met three and a half months later and during a leisurely meal in a hotel I shared with him my most interesting discoveries.

Towards the end of the 1913 lock-out and strike, with the Dublin workers and the trade-union movement in disarray, Larkin, despite the objections of colleagues, left for a lecture tour in the US. His proposed visit lasted more than nine years and he missed out on the Easter 1916 Rising and the war of independence. On his return to Ireland he attempted unsuccessfully to regain control of the Irish Transport and General Workers Union. Thereafter he led a campaign of vilification against the leadership of the labour movement, much of it directed at Thomas Johnson and William O'Brien. And for most of the rest of his life he was the centre of bitter internecine strife in the trade-union movement and the Labour Party, which for decades thwarted the attempts of the labour movement to be a major influence in Irish politics.

Larkin's treatment of Johnson was vindictive. During the general election in September 1927 he spent most of his time attacking the Labour leader. He and his supporters followed Johnson around the latter's County Dublin constituency and when the Labour leader attempted to address meetings shouted him down. Not least because of the intervention of Larkin and his supporters in the election campaign, and the consequent disarray in their ranks, the Labour Party retained only 13 of their 22 seats. Larkin's display of antipathy to Johnson, the mildest of men, was not limited to the hustings. Whenever he met him in the street he publicly abused him.

John Feeney's article on the interview appeared in the *Evening Herald* 9 October 1979. Under the headings, 'Study that will shock trade unionists' and 'Larkin, a wrecker and a demagogue', it was designed to be sensational and was clearly going to be so. The prevailing attitude to Larkin at that time was totally uncritical. In *Strumpet City*, a novel centred on the 1913 strike, James Plunkett Kelly had captured Larkin's charisma and the manner in which he had inspired workers to organise and insist on their rights. RTÉ had produced and shown a most popular TV series adapted from the novel, with Peter O'Toole playing 'Big Jim'. And the labour movement had had a statue of Larkin erected in O'Connell Street, where he could be seen with such giants of Irish history as Daniel O'Connell and Charles Stewart Parnell.

I was not comfortable with the extent to which John had hyped-up the interview but as there was nothing in the piece that was not factual I was not unduly worried. However, at noon on the day following the publication of John's article I had a phone call from Vinnie Doyle, editor of the *Evening Herald*, and Michael Brophy, the assistant editor. They were on a common line and both were agitated. It seems that a few hours earlier a large trade-union delegation had arrived at the *Irish Independent* newspaper offices and caused the staff to stop work. The management was told that, until there was a full apology for, and detailed retraction of, the article, work would not be resuming in the newspaper offices.

John Feeney, with his occasional baiting-style of journalism, had for quite some time been causing considerable stress to his editorial colleagues so when Vinnie Doyle threatened to sack him I insisted that I was mainly responsible for the offending article. I drafted a letter of apology with the help of Donal Nevin, assistant secretary to the Irish Congress of Trade Unions, and the trade-union delegation was somewhat mollified. The editor further guaranteed that John, who had conveniently taken a few days' leave, would on his return publish an article which would vindicate the high regard in which Larkin was held by the Irish people. This was enough to end the walk-out.

The incident at the Independent newspaper offices was featured on the front page of the *Irish Press* together with comments from Denis Larkin, TD, who dismissed my assessment of his father as rubbish. On that day also I was interviewed about my view of Jim Larkin and my forthcoming book on the RTÉ news bulletin at 1 p.m.. Three days later John Feeney's promised profile of Larkin appeared. It was so close to hagiography as to be ironic. There were two further ironies. When interviewed on RTÉ about the forthcoming book, apart from having drafted extensive notes, I had not begun to write even the first chapter. And, later when the book had been launched at Listowel's Writers' Week in July 1980, it was favourably reviewed by academics and leading members of the labour movement, none of whom registered the slightest complaint about the treatment of Jim Larkin. At that time also I was a member of the Irish Labour History Society and the incident in no way affected my friendship with two of the Society's most prominent members, Paul Cullen, the treasurer, or Francis Devine who lectured at the ITGWU training and educational college at Palmerston Park, Rathmines.

John Feeney and I remained friends. A brilliant journalist, he was something of an anarchist, and with immense courage, attacked injustice wherever he found it. Much read and discussed, he was in the vanguard of the new confrontational and controversial style of journalism which had been adopted by the practitioners of the print media to cope with the fierce competition they were experiencing from radio, television and the British tabloids. John was as equally opposed to totalitarian regimes of the left as to those of the right and his saving grace was that he was always on the side of the underdog. I was glad I was able to show my regard for John by assisting at his obsequies after he died in an air crash.

An author generally draws attention to his or her book by having it formally launched, discussing it during a radio or TV interview and

by reviews in journals, newspapers or radio and TV book programmes. Up to about ten years ago book launches were generously
covered by the press. Latterly, for the most part, only the launch of
books by celebrities, established writers and journalists are noted in
the media. Thus the book launch has become almost an exercise in
self-indulgence.

Until it fell out of favour with the press I found the book launch
most useful. I was greatly indebted to my friend, Mary Moloney, for
advice on how to organise one. Mary was a highly respected journalist and sub-editor with the *Irish Press* Group. From her I learned,
among other things, that the ideal time for a book launch was 7 or
7.30 on Tuesday evening, when the newspapers would have cleared
most topical stories over the weekend. She also emphasised the importance of providing an informative summary of the book to be
launched and a biographical note on its author.

Normally the greatest worry for a publisher and author before a
book-launch is that copies of the book might not be available on time.
With only a few exceptions this was the case in those which I organised. Other difficulties can and do arise. I had to face quite a few when
launching *Austin Stack: portrait of a separatist*.

León Ó Broin, the writer and historian, had agreed to launch the
book. I had become acquainted with him while researching in the
National Library of Ireland, where we occasionally shared information. However, five days before the launch he was confined to bed
with flu. Fortunately I was able to have Bishop James Kavanagh
deputise for him.

I decided to have the launch in Collins Barracks. This I did on the
invitation to my friend, Commandant Patrick D. O'Donnell, who
then had responsibility for the barrack's mess. A month or so earlier
Paddy had *The Irish faction-fighters of the nineteenth century* launched
there. He told me he had been prompted to write this book by the
list of sources on the subject which I had included in my history of
North Kerry. When I disclosed my intention to have the book-launch
in Collins Barracks, Mrs Nanette Barrett told me she could not agree
with a book on Austin Stack being launched in a barracks named after

Michael Collins! The Stack family solved this difficulty by volunteering to organise the launch in the Central Hotel, off Harcourt Street.

At 2 a.m. on the morning of the launch I was faced by a much more serious difficulty. Nanette telephoned to check that all preparations were in place for the launch. She told me she had met Seán MacBride and that he had accepted her invitation to the launch. Apart from having been honoured with the Nobel Peace Prize and the Lenin Peace Prize, in his early years he had been a friend and comrade of Austin Stack in the Republican movement. I had scarcely ended telling her how pleased I was that he was coming to the launch when she added that she had also met and invited Daithí Ó Conaill. At that time he was alleged to be the chief of staff of the Provisional IRA and was 'on the run'. The Provisionals' campaign was at its most intense so it was not a time to be irresponsible. I told Nanette I was horrified at the suggestion and that she should tell him it was in no one's interests that he attend. Nanette ended the conversation by reminding me that Daithí had no forwarding address!

I did not sleep very well that night. I was appalled by the prospect of Bishop James Kavanagh being very seriously embarrassed. A short time previously he had mediated in a difficult situation involving 'Provos' and a malicious rumour had been circulated that he was unduly sympathetic to them. I was also worried at the adverse effect that the reported presence of the activists would have on the reputations of the rest of those attending the book launch, not least Senator Ruadhrí Brugha and his wife Máire. Daughter of Terence MacSweeney, Máire had given me on loan her aunt Mary's papers which had been most valuable in my research.

When I arrived at the Central Hotel for the book launch I was met by Austin Stack. A nephew of the subject of the biography, he was a mild-mannered proprietor of a travel business in Terenure. In some agitation he told me that Daithí Ó Conaill, Joe Cahill, the editor of *An Phoblacht* and a number of other prominent Republicans were in the bar. Despite his remonstrations, he told me they were determined to attend the book launch and added: 'Fr. You are about the only one who might be able to stop them.'

I delivered a parcel of books to the room upstairs where the book launch was to be held. As I returned downstairs to the bar I decided that the only way out of the quandary was to have the official/press launch and reception at 7.30 and a second one for the family and friends at 8.30. In the bar I asked to speak with Joe Cahill. I reminded him that when the dependants of the internees in Northern Ireland were in need I had not been found wanting. He and his companions, I assured him, were most welcome to the launch and 'planned' reception for family and friends at 8.30. Joe and Daithí Ó Conaill, who had joined him, protested that they had been invited but I succeeded in persuading them that it was not in my interest or theirs that they be present for the press launch and reception.

To ensure that none of the journalists or invited guests strayed into the bar Austin Stack and another person stood at the hotel entrance and directed them to the book launch. In the event between 7.30 and 8 Bishop James Kavanagh arrived and formally launched the book. The journalists and photographers had a number of assignments to cover. They rushed in and after listening to Bishop Kavanagh, collected the handouts, took their pictures and promptly left. At 8.30 Daithí Ó Conaill and 'the folk downstairs', as Austin Stack described them, came into the room. I presented him with a signed copy of the book. He was very tall, handsome, quietly-spoken and pleasant. I was surprised at how relaxed he and his companions appeared to be.

My attempt to stave off public embarrassment was not entirely successful. Lochlinn MacGlynn, Dublin correspondent of the *Kerryman*, had been informed that prominent Republicans would be attending the book launch. He stayed on for the second session. Over a week later his report in the *Kerryman* began by stating that Republicans of all hues and all generations attended the book launch and in listing them he gave pride of place to the then current activists.

For some time I had been attempting to obtain permission from the minister for justice to erect a plaque on Listowel Garda station in connection with an RIC mutiny in June 1920. My friend and classmate at St Michael's College, Gerard Lynch, Fine Gael TD for North Kerry, had not been able to obtain the permission from his colleague,

1. Writers' Week, 1971. *Left to right*: Séamus Wilmot, John B. Keane, Bryan MacMahon, Marie Keane and Timothy Danaher

2. Writers' Week, 1978. *Left to right*: Eleanor Scanlon, the Honourable Desmond Fitz-Gerald, knight of Glin, Mrs Kit Aherne, TD, Mrs Maureen Beasley and Father J. Anthony Gaughan

3. Writers' Week, 1986, with Desmond O'Malley, TD

4.

Sir Adrian FitzGerald, 6th baronet and 24th knight of Kerry

Right Honourable William Francis Hare, 5th earl of Listowel

Charles E. Kelly

Edward MacLysaght

John J. Synon

Judge Dermot Kinlen

5. *Above*: Launch of *The crucified* at the exhibition centre, Bank of Ireland, 1985, with Archbishop Kevin McNamara and Cardinal Tomás Ó Fiaich   6. *Left*: Signing a book for Donncha Ó Dúlaing at the same launch

7. Con Murphy replying to the launch of *Alfred O'Rathilly I* in Newman House, 1986, with *left to right*: President Patrick J. Hillery, Mrs Maeve Hillery and Jack Lynch, former Taoiseach

8. Launch of *Alfred O'Rathilly III, Pt 2* at Blackrock College, 1993, with Rev Professor Patrick J. Corish and Dr T.K. Whittaker

9. Launch of *Olivia Mary Taaffe* by Cardinal Cahal B. Daly in 1995, at head office of St Josephs' Young Priests Society, with Eileen Sparling, president of the Society

10. Annual P.E.N. dinner at Nieve's Restaurant, Dalkey, 1981. *Left to right*: Fr J. Anthony Gaughan, Gordon Thomas, Charles J. Haughey, TD, Sam McAughtry and Arthur Flynn

11. Annual P.E.N. dinner at National Yacht Club, Dún Laoghaire, 1996. *Left to right*: Arthur Flynn, Margaret Neylon, O.Z. Whitehead, President Mary Robinson, Sheila Flitton, Fr J. Anthony Gaughan, Marita Conlon McKenna and Krzysztof Romanowski

12. Presentation of the A.T. Cross/Irish P.E.N. literary award, 2000. *Left to right*: Brian Friel, Fr J. Anthony Gaughan and Séamus Heaney

13. Presentation of the A.T. Cross/Irish P.E.N. literary award at the National Yacht Club, Dún Laoghaire, 2001. *Left to right*: Paul Gibney, Edna O'Brien, President Mary McAleese, Arthur Flynn, Fr J. Anthony Gaughan and Mrs Nesta Tuomey

14. Presentation of the A.T. Cross/Irish P.E.N. literary award, at the Beaufield Mews Restaurant, 2002. *Left to right*: William Trevor, Maeve Binchy, Fr J. Anthony Gaughan and Gordon Snell

15. Group of boy scouts on roof of St Peter's Basilica, Rome, 1950. *Front row, left to right*: Tim Lyons, John Kennelly, Niall Stack, Tony Gaughan and Dan Maher. *Back row, left to right*: Matt Kennelly, Maurice Kennelly, Michael Kennelly, Séamus Buckley and Patsy Bolster

16. With Kenneth McGowan and Éamon Mac Thomáis at a book launch in 1985

17. With Brother Thomas O'Grady, OH, *2nd from left*, Fr Kevin Doheny, CSSp, *3rd from left* and staff at the Refugee Trust centre in Sarajevo, 1996

Paddy Cooney. After a change of government I was on the point of receiving this from Gerry Collins, through the good offices of Mrs Kit Aherne, TD. I was worried about the effect MacGlynn's report might have on the minister and his advisers. I explained the situation to him in a personal letter and replied to MacGlynn's report in the *Kerryman*. Gerry Collins agreed to see me at his clinic in Abbeyfeale and after stoically sitting through a lecture that I should not be 'running around with the Provos' I was relieved to receive the permission.

When advising me on how to organise a book launch Mary Moloney stressed the importance of the location which should be in the city centre, accessible and 'interesting'. The location of two of my book launches had this last quality. The appearance of *The knights of Glin* coincided with a fund-raising event promoted by the Irish Georgian Society. This was held in the residence of the US ambassador in the Phoenix Park. Desmond Fitz-Gerald had little difficulty in persuading the Honourable Desmond Guinness, president of the Society, to include the launch of the book on his family as part of the evening's events.

William (Bill) Shannon, the US ambassador, was a respected academic and author. His wife, Elizabeth, subsequently wrote a charming account of her experience in Ireland, entitled *Up in the park*. The company at the function was most congenial and Elizabeth Shannon launched *The knights of Glin*. It seems that virtually everybody present bought a copy of the book and this first issue was sold out in less than three months. Subsequently that other book of mine, a biography of Tom Johnson, leader of the Labour Party, was widely read but its sale was much slower. As a result I tended to divide people into two categories: those who bought books and did not read them and those who read books but did not buy them. A close friend a fellow curate in Monkstown, Fr Bertie Moore, belonged to the first category. Whenever I published a new book he would say: 'Tony, I don't mind buying a copy as long as you don't expect me to read it'.

When I told Dermot Kinlen that I was looking around for a location in which to launch my biography of his grandfather, Judge Tom O'Donnell, he immediately suggested that we have the launch in his residence. Situated in Merrion Road, his home is a house of generous proportions. He told me he was eager also to avail of the occasion to host a social evening for his many friends. Jack Lynch, the former Taoiseach, was at his most urbane in launching the book. He described how he had begun his working life as an official in the Cork circuit court in December 1936. At that time O'Donnell was a judge in that court and, it seems, was particularly friendly to him and encouraged him to study law and further his career.

Between 1985 and 1993 I published *The crucified* by Alfred O'Rahilly and a four-volume biography of that remarkable polymath. I was acutely aware of how crucial a successful launch of these books would be to promote interest in them. In the event I had extraordinary good fortune in this regard. Through the good offices of Con Murphy, Ellen Lynch (later Mrs Dave Hegarty) generously volunteered to handle the publicity in connection with the launching of these books.

As competent as she was beautiful, Ellen was a key person in the PR section of the head office of the Bank of Ireland. She insisted that the top churchman in the country was the person to launch the book and, at my request, Cardinal Tomás Ó Fiaich generously agreed to do so. He was joined by Archbishop Kevin McNamara who had a short time previously been transferred from Kerry to Dublin. Ellen left nothing to chance. She even insisted that I take an afternoon nap so as to look fresh and 'perky' at the launch! Not least because of her efforts a report and/or picture of the launch appeared in all the daily and the two evening newspapers on the following day.

For the launch of *Alfred O'Rahilly, I: academic* Ellen chose Newman House, St Stephen's Green, where some of the rooms after a recent refurbishing were at their most elegant. T.K. Whitaker, chancellor of the National University of Ireland, who had provided a foreword to the book, conducted the launch. Newman House was again the location for the launch of *Alfred O'Rahilly II: public figure*. President Patrick J. Hillery and his wife, Maeve, were the principal guests with the president sending the book on its way. At the launch Proinsias MacAonghusa, an ever helpful friend, slyly whispered to me that having Hillery launch a book with a foreword by Haughey must be one of my greatest achievements to date. He implied this also in his report on the launch. It was only in retrospect that I became aware of the significance of his remark.

The third volume dealt with O'Rahilly as a sociologist and more importantly as a social activist and reformer. The department of extra-mural studies was one of the legacies O'Rahilly left to UCC. Although this would have been the most appropriate location for the launch, I had to settle for the head office of the ESB. In presiding, Bishop James Kavanagh paid a well-deserved tribute to O'Rahilly's achievement in pioneering University-sponsored adult education in Ireland. The final volume, O'Rahilly as a Catholic apologist, was launched by Monsignor Patrick Corish. The venue was Blackrock College which was truly for O'Rahilly an *alma mater*. Having begun his education in the college he spent his retirement years there as a guest of the Holy Ghost Fathers.

By the mid-1990s, as far as I was concerned, the book-launch was no longer useful for drawing attention to a book. However I did launch two further books. I had prepared for publication *Olivia Mary Taaffe (1882-1918): foundress of St Joseph's Young Priests Society* as part of the Society's centenary celebrations in 1995. It was launched by Cardinal Cahal B. Daly to mark the re-opening of the Society's head office after extensive renovations. And, at the organising committee's request, I had Martin Mansergh launch *Memoirs of Senator Joseph Connolly: a founder of modern Ireland* at Listowel's Writers' Week 1996.

The book review, favourable or otherwise, is crucial in order to excite the interest of the reading public and, most of all, that of book-sellers and librarians. In seeking to have books reviewed over a period of more than thirty years I have found the literary editors of the news-papers unfailingly helpful. This was especially the case with those who had responsibility for the book pages of the newspapers of the *Irish Press* Group and Dick Roche of the *Irish Independent* and John Banville of the *Irish Times*. I have never aimed at obtaining a good review but rather to have my books reviewed by academics, writers and journalists who had won the respect of their peers. Of the many distinguished persons I asked to review a book none refused and only a few failed to do so. Cardinal Cahal B. Daly was one of the latter. Subsequently when he provided a superb foreword to *At the coal face: recollections of a city and country priest 1950-2000* he was at pains to point out that he now felt he had discharged a debt of honour!

CHAPTER 7

Member of Irish P.E.N.

I joined Irish P.E.N. in January 1974. This I did at the request of John B. Keane, who served as its president from 1973 to 1977. Irish P.E.N. is a branch of International P.E.N., a worldwide association of writers. P.E.N. brings together poets, novelists, essayists, historians, playwrights, critics, translators, editors, journalists and screenwriters in a common concern for the craft of writing, and a commitment to freedom of expression and the promotion of international good will. Through its 129 centres in more than 90 countries, it operates on all continents.

It was founded in London in 1921 by novelist Catherine Amy Dawson Scott. She sent the following notice to potential members: 'London has no centre where well-known writers of both sexes can meet, no place where visitors from abroad can hope to find them. A dinner club would enable them to meet socially without being under obligation to anyone . . . The qualifications for membership are: (a) A book of verse published by a well-known continental, London or

American firm; (b) A play produced by any well-known theatre; (c) The editorship, past or present, of a well-known newspaper or magazine; (d) A novel published by a well-known London, continental or American firm. Membership subscription 5/- [five shillings] yearly'.

The forty-one writers who attended the inaugural dinner at a restaurant in Piccadilly on 5 October 1921 joined the new P.E.N. club, Thereafter they were known as the 'Foundation Members' and among them were Joseph Conrad, John Galsworthy and D.H. Lawrence. Later, prominent writers in continental Europe and North America were approached with a view to establishing centres in their own countries. The response from most of them, including Maxim Gorky in Russia, Anatole France in France and Edith Wharton in the US, was positive and soon the organisation became international with its administrative centre in London.

Marjorie Watts, P.E.N.'s first secretary and daughter of its founder, wrote to Lady Augusta Gregory in Dublin suggesting that she summon writers together to form a centre in Ireland. This attempt to establish a P.E.N. centre in Ireland with Lady Gregory as president was not entirely successful. It seems that Irish writers were in the main solitary characters, not prone to joining organisations or discussing their work. This attitude was not uncommon among the best-known writers. When George Bernard Shaw was invited to preside at an English P.E.N. dinner his reply was typically Shavian: 'Galsworthy was pulling your leg. He knows that I abhor literary society. As to presiding at a literary dinner words fail me! You can't really have enjoyed that foolish crowd at Stratford'. But Shaw joined P.E.N. in 1924 yielding to John Galsworthy's persuasion as follows: 'Whitemailer! Very well, I will go quietly. It's your doing, though, but I will not face a recurrent irritation of a guinea a year, Here is twenty guineas for a life subscription (I am 68). If they won't accept that they can make me an honorary member, and be damned to them'.

The second attempt to establish a P.E.N. centre in Ireland was more successful. In 1934 this was spearheaded by Bulmer Hobson, Lord Longford and Seán Ó Faoláin. Joint centres were set up in Belfast and Dublin thus providing a link between Irish writers north and south. By 1940 Irish P.E.N. had over 130 members, more than a hundred belonging to the Dublin centre.

Most of the best-known Irish writers since then have been members of P.E.N. including: John Banville, Maeve Binchy, Clare Boylan, Brian Cleeve, Fr Desmond Forristal, Monk Gibbon, Jennifer Johnston, Mary Lavin, J.J. Lee, Walter Macken, Edward MacLysaght, Bryan MacMahon, Brinsley MacNamara, Conor Cruise O'Brien, Edna O'Brien, Kate O'Brien, Frank O'Connor, Peader O'Donnell, Liam O'Flaherty, Francis Stuart, Alice Taylor, and Maurice Walsh. Playwrights have been represented by Maurice Davin Power, Bernard Farrell, Brian Friel, Denis Johnston, John B. Keane, Hugh Leonard and Frank McGuinness. And the names of poets such as Eavan Boland, Austin Clarke, John F. Deane and Séamus Heaney are also on the rolls of Irish P.E.N.

Not having a premises of its own Irish P.E.N. has had to conduct meetings at various venues. Initially meetings were held in Roberts literary café in Grafton Street. Later they were held in the office of *Dublin Opinion* and in a meeting room of the Royal Dublin Society. For the most part, appropriately enough, they have been and are still held in the United Arts Club. In the 1940s and 1950s meetings were occasionally convened in the homes of members of the executive committee, following a sherry reception.

One of the most memorable dates in the early history of Irish P.E.N. was 27 June 1935, when the centre organised a dinner on the seventieth birthday of W.B. Yeats. The venue was the Hibernian Hotel, where the ballroom was transformed into a banqueting hall. One press report described Yeats with his white mane sitting serenely at the top table listening to an address by John Masefield, the poet laureate of England. The toast was to 'Ireland and Yeats' and glowing tributes were paid by his contemporaries.

Ireland has been the location for the International P.E.N. Congress in 1953 and 1971. The latter assembly met on the golden jubilee of the association and its theme was 'The changing face of literature: a discussion and evaluation of developments over the past fifty years'. Five hundred delegates attended the congress in the Royal Marine Hotel,

Dún Laoghaire. The Taoiseach, Jack Lynch, at the opening ceremony described the gathering as 'a world assembly of men and women of letters' and recalled that, when P.E.N. was founded, Dublin was the centre of a remarkable literary revival; 'Synge was only a few years dead, Yeats was at the height of his power and Joyce was putting the finishing touches to *Ulysses*'. In his closing address the international president, Heinrich Boll, paid an exceptionally warm tribute to Irish P.E.N. for their successful organisation of the congress.

Irish P.E.N. has fought for many causes. Censorship in general and the censorship of books in particular were ever-recurring themes for discussion at meetings. The centre took a strong line against a strange ban on the importation of Irish books into England. It lobbied against the imposition of VAT on books and, with others, successfully sought for legislation to ensure that writers would be paid for the use of their books in libraries. Irish P.E.N. petitioned the Taoiseach to introduce a pension scheme for artists, writers and poets who had fallen on bad times, similar to the Aosdána arrangement which was eventually inaugurated. It campaigned to ensure that the tax exemption granted to writers was continued. Occasionally it became involved in issues concerning copyright.

I was elected to the executive committee of Irish P.E.N. in May 1976. Charles E. Kelly was both chairman and president. He had held many senior posts in the civil service, including that of director of broadcasting. But he will always be associated with *Dublin Opinion*.

This satirical monthly was founded by Arthur Booth in 1922. Following his death Charlie Kelly with Tom Collins co-edited it from 1926 to 1968. Many of the cartoons in *Dublin Opinion* were brilliant but CEK, as Charlie signed his work, had a niche of his own in social commentary. Even up to the 1970s people recalled their favourite CEK cartoons. There was the depiction of the night that the Kildare Street Club held a *céilí*. Charlie had lots of fun with the diminutive Séan T. O'Kelly. The latter in a speech after the 1938 Anglo-Irish Agreement which ended the so-called 'Economic War' claimed publicly that we had 'whipped John Bull'. For a long time afterwards Charlie depicted him with a whip hanging out of his back pocket. He presented an elongated de Valera/'the Long Fellow' with a sly and mis-chievous gleam in his eye. His cartoon on the cover of *Dublin Opinion* for August 1942, which reflected the widespread influence of Alfred O'Rahilly's sustained and occasional intemperate attacks on the Central Bank Bill, had the hallmark of genius.

Charlie's humour and that of the *Dublin Opinion* was a satire in words and drawings which had bite but little or no rancour. It laughed at the Irish Free State's new institutions and political bodies and it laughed with them. Although in the early years of the new State there was much to be grateful for and much hope expressed, there was also a confusion and a great deal of strife and hatred, arising from the civil war. In that context the appearance of the saucy *Dublin Opinion* and Charlie's cartoons were more than timely when it was important to help Ireland laugh and laugh in a wholesome way.

It has frequently been stated that many of those who write and perform comedy are sad and lonely people. At meetings of P.E.N. Charlie was always in high good humour and obviously a person who enjoyed company. But I was surprised at how seldom he indulged in humorous exchanges or repartee.

Desmond Clarke and Barbara Walsh, as members of the commit-tee, did more than most in terms of organisation. Desmond was the librarian at the RDS and had acted as secretary to Irish P.E.N. for many years. Barbara was the treasurer. Subsequently they exchanged roles. It was generally recognised that Desmond and Barbara were responsible for the remarkable success of the Irish centre's golden jubilee congress and celebrations.

Dorine Rohan had her career as a writer and her membership of the committee cut short by a horrific accident which left her seriously disabled. Constantine FitzGibbon, an expatriate American, attended meetings only occasionally and, it seemed to me, generally after a pro-tracted lunch. Alan Llewellyn was an eccentric Welshman. A very large man, he had an extraordinarily high-pitched voice and tended to be over-sensitive.

Rita O'Brien had spent a lifetime promoting the arts. She was as interested in the visual arts as she was in literature and had established an art gallery near the former Hell Fire Club in the Dublin mountains which had a cult status for a number of years.

Irene Haugh, Mary Lavin and Eithne Strong also served on the committee. Of these Mary Lavin was the best known, mainly for her short stories. There was the poet, John F. Deane. Tall, with thin features, he had a long beard and the appearance of an ascetic. By contrast John Ryan's appearance left us in no doubt that he was a bon vivant. Better known as a broadcaster than as a writer, he was at the time attempting to launch a literary magazine.

For me the most interesting member of the committee was Bryan Walter Guinness. He was the oldest son of Walter Edward Guinness, first Baron Moyne. In 1944 he had succeeded his father as second Baron Moyne and was known as Lord Moyne. He had had a few books of poetry published and was respected as a poet. At meetings he was rather quaintly referred to as Moyne.

Although he was well able to hold his ground in argument, he was a gentle and very likeable person. In the late 1970s and early 1980s the conflict in Northern Ireland was becoming more and more tragic. On a number of occasions I proposed that Irish P.E.N. should take a public stand in the matter and, in effect, urge the British authorities to aim for a political rather than a military solution to the civil unrest and at times open warfare. In the event, most of the members of the committee were opposed to any public intervention on the grounds that it would mean straying into the area of politics which was not countenanced in the constitution of P.E.N. So Irish P.E.N. maintained a silence on the subject.

On the occasions on which this matter was discussed Moyne cogently and vigorously argued a counter-view to mine. After two such sessions he invited me to continue the discussion over lunch at his imposing residence, 'Knockmaroon House', near Chapelizod. These occasions were more convivial than when Moyne, in conjunction with Irish P.E.N., hosted a special tribute evening for the distinguished writer, Liam O'Flaherty, on the latter's 85th birthday.

Apart from Irish P.E.N., Lord Moyne was involved in other cultural activities. He was a prominent member of the Irish Association for Cultural, Economic and Social Relations. Under its aegis a group drawn from Britain, Northern Ireland and the Republic of Ireland met to promote co-operation and good-will between the three jurisdictions. Their meetings were held in London, Belfast and in the Friendly Club, St Stephen's Green, Dublin.

When Lord Moyne had read my biography of Tom Johnson he invited me to give a talk to the group on the Labour leader. Apart from being flattered by the invitation, I was immensely gratified that the event was a cause of considerable pleasure to Mrs Kathleen Johnson, Tom Johnson's daughter-in-law. Kathleen was the manager of the bar in the Friendly Club. Throughout her life she had been closer to Johnson than even his wife, Marie, and she was delighted that the achievements and stature of 'Pops', as she referred to him, were being discussed in such influential company.

Lord Moyne continued to be a member of the executive committee of Irish P.E.N. until mid-1985, when, owing to ill-health, he resigned. However, I was fortunate to have a signed copy of his poems which he had presented to me to remember him by.

CHAPTER 8

Chairman of Irish P.E.N.

In April 1981 I was elected chairman of the executive committee of Irish P.E.N. which by that time represented only the Dublin Centre. Owing to the serious civil unrest in Northern Ireland, the Belfast Centre had been dormant from 1974 onwards and eventually in 1977 it had been disbanded and some of its members had joined the Dublin Centre. Also in 1981 Arthur Flynn became the honorary secretary of Irish P.E.N. As interested in the theatre as in literature, Arthur was already a member of the Society of Irish Playwrights and from 1985 onwards has served as treasurer of that Society which in 2001 became the Screen Writers and Playwrights Guild. Apart from his writing and deep interest in film-making in Ireland, Arthur mainly concerned himself with drafting plays for radio. For more than two decades, by virtue of his diligence and organisational skill, he has been largely responsible for the successful running of Irish P.E.N.

The principal activity of the Centre is the monthly meeting open to members, associate members and the public. This follows a meeting of the committee and generally is a presentation from a member of the committee, an author who has just had a book published or a playwright whose play has recently been produced. Over the years there have been some memorable lectures: Barry Cassin on his reminiscences of the Irish theatre, Pat Donlon on the National Library of Ireland, Chris Fitzsimons on Hilton Edwards and Mícheál MacLiamóir, Marian Keaney on Padraic Colum, Gus Martin and Lorna Reynolds on Yeats and David Norris on Joyce. Talent as a writer is no guarantee that a person will be an interesting public speaker. Lectures by the immensely successful writers: Ian St James and Gordon Thomas, promised more than they fulfilled. On those occasions the humanity and personality of the lecturers is much to the fore. I recall Garret FitzGerald, when talking about his then recently published *All in a life*, making some extraordinary claims and comments about his very early childhood.

The average attendance at meetings is just under 20. On occasion the committee has been embarrassed by the small number who have come to a lecture by a well-known writer. Only two members of the public arrived for a lecture by Peter de Rosa. A few years earlier he had given a well-attended lecture and had returned to speak on his new publication *Rebels: the Irish rising of 1916* (1990). Aware of the embarrassment of the committee, before he began he recalled that some fifteen years earlier, when involved in an extramural university course, he had been deputed to travel from the south of England to the University of Hull to deliver a lecture. Two persons attended and he learned afterwards that one of them was stone-deaf!

The Centre generally has as many associate members as members who are established writers. In May 2001 it had 87 members and 77 associates. Thus one of its aims is to encourage and help aspiring writers. Apart from authors discussing their work, sessions are held on 'How to get published?' Representatives from the publishing houses attend and reply to queries on every aspect of their trade. Without exception publishers and writers' agents have been generous with their support in this regard. And at different times Michael Gill, Michael O'Brien and the affable Seán O'Boyle of Columba Press have represented publishers on the committee of Irish P.E.N.

'The role of the critic' has been discussed with the help of literary and theatre critics. Theatre directors have explained the relationship between the playwright and a director in the presentation of a play. And to promote cultural events the Centre has from time to time joined with other groups, such as the Canadian Embassy, Dublin City of Culture Committee, Dublin Millennium Cultural Committee and the Goethe Institute.

The Centre also encourages aspiring writers by the sponsorship of prizes under its aegis. From 1983 until his death in 1996 O.Z. Whitehead, a member of the committee, presented an annual prize of £500 to the winner of a play competition. Since 1996 this competition has been funded by Carolyn Swift. For a number of years a Peace Prize, valued at £350, was sponsored by Associate Member Mrs Eileen Healy. The prize was for a short story on the theme of peace. When this sponsorship lapsed it was renewed for a number of years by Ian St James.

The Centre is honoured to be associated with the most prestigious literary prize of all: that presented by the Nobel Peace Committee in Stockholm. The committee is invited to nominate a writer for that prize. It is now no secret that Séamus Heaney almost invariably was the Centre's choice. When Heaney was awarded the Nobel Prize for Literature in 1995 the Centre in its letter of congratulation offered him honorary life membership of Irish P.E.N. which he graciously accepted.

In 1998 the Centre initiated its own prize: the A.T. Cross/Irish P.E.N. annual award. This award, restricted to Irish-born writers, is presented to those who have made an outstanding contribution to Irish writing. During a discussion by the committee on the Nobel Prize for Literature it was generally agreed that it was unlikely that that prize would be coming again to Ireland in the near future. Krzysztof J. Romanowski informed the meeting that in his native Poland an annual award presented by Polish P.E.N. was regarded as second only in prestige to the Nobel Prize. His suggestion that Irish P.E.N. should present such an award was enthusiastically endorsed.

A.T. Cross, the pen manufacturer, sponsored the prize and it was presented in 1999 to John B. Keane, in 2000 to Brian Friel, in 2001 to Edna O'Brien and in 2002 to William Trevor.

The administrative centre in London of International P.E.N. keeps national Centres informed of events which affect writers in different parts of the world. In addition, at the Annual International Congress academics and writers from across the world discuss issues relevant to all writers and writing. When the Congress is held outside Europe it has not been possible for Irish P.E.N. to be represented, largely because of the cost involved. However, when it has been convened in Europe, Ireland has been represented. In 1981 John F. Deane attended the Congress which was jointly held in Lyon and Paris, in 1981 and 1988 Arthur Flynn represented the Irish Centre at London and Cambridge respectively and in 1994 Dr Maria Romanowski on behalf of the committee attended the Congress in Prague.

The 66th World Congress was held in the University of Warsaw in June 1999. Delegates from more than 70 countries attended. With Krzysztof J. and Maria Romanowski I represented Irish P.E.N. At the request of the committee I prepared a report on the Congress to be circulated to members (for this, see Appendix 1).

At every Congress writers who have been imprisoned because of the expression of their ideas and views are always an important item on the agenda. However it is not only at Congress that this topic is given priority. In almost all correspondence from the International Centre to national Centres there is news about these writers and the efforts of members of P.E.N. to have them released or at least to draw public attention to their plight.

In 1986 Irish P.E.N. set up a sub-committee to improve its support for these prisoners of conscience. Aisling Ní Dhonnchadha was most active in this campaign. A lecturer in the department of Irish in Our Lady of Mercy College of Education at Carysfort, Blackrock, and already a member of Amnesty International, she corresponded with prisoners and even succeeded in sending books to some of them. One of her correspondents had received a sentence of 48 years for writing articles!

In the series Beocheist in the *Irish Times* of 8 May 1986 Aisling set out the urgency of this campaign. She noted that, according to the report issued in the previous autumn by the Writers in Prison Committee of International P.E.N., 445 writers, editors or publishers were either in jail, prison camps or detained in mental institutions. Still others had simply disappeared, as a result of the determination of governments or rulers to stifle freedom of speech and the publication of the truth. She gave the main outlines of three writers who had been imprisoned: Alaide F. de Salorzano in Guatemala, Recep Marashi in Turkey and Lothar Herbst in Poland. She added that there were hundreds of similar cases in Russia, Iran, Cuba and Vietnam. Aisling quoted Nadine Gordimer: 'All the writer can do, as a writer, is to go on writing the truth as he or she sees it'. She concluded by quoting Camus and Voltaire on the obligation of all writers to speak on behalf of writers and people who were prevented from 'speaking out'.

Down through the years the prisoners Irish P.E.N. attempted to assist were in Cuba, South Africa, Taiwan, Turkey and Uruguay. When Aisling resigned from P.E.N. in 1991 her active concern for prisoners of conscience was continued by Susan Schreibmann. A native of New York and lecturer in the department of English in UCD, her chief interest was prisoners in Cuba.

In 1990 the Centre organised the collection and transport to Romania of much needed books after the fall of the communist regime of Nicolae Ceaucescu. In 1991, like every other Centre throughout the world, Irish P.E.N. protested to the Iranian government about the fatwah/death threat pronounced on Salman Rushdie. This followed protests which had been made by the Centre in the spring of 1989.

Towards the end of 1990 Gerry Adams, the leading spokesperson for Sinn Féin, applied for membership of Irish P.E.N. Traditionally the requirement for membership has been either (a) two books published professionally, (b) two plays produced professionally or (c) a book and play from each of these categories (for the rules of Irish P.E.N., see Appendix 2). In due course a completed form, including a listing of two books, *Falls memories* (1982) and *The politics of Irish freedom* (1986), published by Brandon Press, and the current membership fee of £10 was received. Some members of the committee were vigorously opposed to Adams becoming a member. I argued strongly that, as he had fulfilled the requirements for membership, he was entitled to it. In the event, a majority of the committee agreed with that point of view and Adams' membership was passed in customary fashion at the monthly meeting in January 1991.

Soon afterwards Adams' membership of Irish P.E.N. was reported in the *Evening Press*. The committee was subjected to considerable adverse criticism on the matter. Hugh Leonard was among those who were most vociferous in their objections. He publicly stated that, as a result, he was resigning from P.E.N., notwithstanding the fact that his membership had lapsed years earlier. He then challenged me to publicly debate the issue with him. I was glad to oblige. On a live-radio programme I explained that Adams had fulfilled the requirements for membership and so was entitled to it. I also pointed out that bans, censorship, the imprisoning of writers for their views were issues on which International P.E.N. took an unambiguous stand. Moreover I pointed out that if Salman Rushdie, who had upset millions with his views, was to apply for membership of Irish P.E.N. he also would be accepted. Leonard's principal counter-argument was to compare Adams to Adolf Hitler!

This did not end the adverse criticism. Considerable pressure was exerted on the secretary of Irish P.E.N. and he contacted the International Centre for advice on the matter. They suggested that Adams should be required to sign the P.E.N. charter. The secretary also learned that Adams had applied to American P.E.N. for permission to enter the US, which he was banned from visiting. The International Centre further stated that they could only support him in his request, if he was giving a talk or attending a writer's conference. Although not unduly surprised, members of the committee were somewhat resentful of the manner in which membership of P.E.N. was being exploited. Nonetheless the matter was left in abeyance and Adams' membership was allowed to stand.

The membership of Gerry Adams became a live issue again in the summer of 1993 with his publisher, Steve MacDonagh of Brandon Press, challenging RTÉ's broadcasting ban on his author and seeking the support of P.E.N. in this regard. By the late autumn, as the outline of the proposals proposed by Gerry Adams and John Hume for a breakthrough in the impasse in Northern Ireland became known, those who were utterly opposed to making any concessions to Sinn Féin exerted considerable pressure to maintain the ban on Adams from broadcasting and other media outlets. Even the International Centre of P.E.N. was lobbied in an attempt to end Adams' continuing membership of Irish P.E.N. and enquired if he had signed the charter. The committee decided to invite him to sign it, but I insisted that all existing members be also asked to do so. For many years this had not been insisted on as a condition for membership. I also undertook to have a message delivered to Adams that, if he wished to remain a member of P.E.N., it was necessary for him to sign the charter promptly! In due course he did so.

At that stage a number of developments were making it impossible to continue the broadcasting and media ban on Sinn Féin and denial of entry to the US to Adams. His membership of P.E.N. was one of these. In retrospect I was glad that in this small way Irish P.E.N. assisted Adams to play his crucial role with John Hume, John Major, George Mitchell, Albert Reynolds and David Trimble in brokering the historic Good Friday Agreement.

CHAPTER 9

Irish P.E.N.'s Main Social Activity

The annual P.E.N. dinner for members and associate members is the highlight of the Centre's events each year. Before 1981 a dinner was held only very occasionally. Soon after he became secretary Arthur Flynn easily persuaded his colleagues on the committee of the merits of such an event, not least in order to raise the public profile of Irish P.E.N. Since then with just one exception the dinner has been held each year and its success has largely been due to the secretary.

At least two visitors are invited to the dinner, one as the guest of honour, the other as principal speaker. Over the years I have felt immensely privileged in acting, with the rest of the committee, as host to a wide variety of distinguished and interesting persons. In November 1981 the guest of honour was Charles J. Haughey, then leader of the Opposition. Both Arthur Flynn and I found Haughey taciturn and seemingly in a rather troubled state of mind. By contrast Sam McAughtry, the principal speaker, was delightful company. At that time McAughtry was writing a column in the *Irish Times* and had for some of the readers almost a cult status.

The venue for the dinner in November 1982 was the Mirabeau Restaurant, near Dún Laoghaire. The proprietor, Seán Kinsella, was a consummate publicist and scarcely a week passed without a report of a local or visiting celebrity dining in the restaurant. The cuisine, it seems, was excellent and the charges exorbitant! Not least because it was probable that a report of the dinner would appear in the press – as indeed it did – Kinsella agreed to provide the P.E.N. dinner at a reasonable price, on condition that the price was not disclosed to anyone. The dinner was excellent and, in his chef's attire, Kinsella welcomed each guest as he or she arrived.

Colm Ó Briain, who had but recently been appointed in charge of the Arts Council, was the guest of honour. In an address which was directed more towards the press than his listeners he set out his plans for the future of the arts in the country. The volatile Dermot Morgan was the principal speaker. A short time earlier I had prepared him and his wife – a Lutheran girl from Hamburg – for their marriage. I reminded him that he owed me a good turn and he kindly agreed to be our principal speaker, even after I cautioned him that there would be no fee.

At that time Morgan was a teacher and was attempting to ease into the entertainment business. He appeared frequently from the audience in Gay Byrne's *Late, Late Show*. He would either do a take on Fr Brian D'Arcy, CP, as 'Fr Trendy' or as a Gaelic League, hurley-wielding troglodyte. In introducing Morgan I attempted to be amusing. Among my remarks I joked that he was with us 'at enormous expense' and I made references to his 'Fr Trendy' and 'Seán, the Gaelic Leaguer and GAA enthusiast'. Morgan did not disappoint and, complete with his hurley, was very entertaining with his routine on the hurley-wielder. However when he sat down he was furious. He accused me of lying about his fee and pointed out that no entertainer or author wishes to be type-cast! Unfortunately I did not improve his mood by suggesting that it was time he grew up.

I had a similar experience on one other occasion. In 1986, as president of Writers' Week, it was my responsibility to introduce Desmond O'Malley, TD, and invite him to open the festival.

During the previous weeks he has been touring the country, urging support for the newly established Progressive Democrats, of which he was a co-founder and leader. His efforts and those of his colleagues had received extraordinarily generous coverage in the media. To lighten my preliminary remarks, I said I was priviledged to introduce a person, some of those present might have heard of. When O'Malley sat down after an effective pitch for his new party, he told me he did not appreciate my brand of humour.

The amiable and unassuming President Patrick J. Hillery and his wife, Maeve, honoured the annual dinner in 1983. The then-promising playwright, Bernard Farrell, was the principal speaker. In the following year Richard Burke, a newly-appointed EC Commissioner, in his grand manner shared with us his vision of the Europe of the future. The guest of honour in 1985 was Cardinal Tomás Ó Fiaich; the principal speaker was Ciaran Carty who after years as literary editor of the *Sunday Independent* had become arts editor of the recently-launched *Sunday Tribune*. The committee was particularly appreciative of the cardinal's presence. Already that day he had attended three public functions and in the small hours intended with his driver to return to Armagh City through the so-called bandit country of South Armagh.

The cardinal was at his jovial best. When I introduced him to Gordon Thomas, the latter invited both of us for lunch during the following week at his residence near Ashford. The cardinal regretted that he would not be free to accept the invitation, but Thomas made me promise that I would. In due course I enjoyed a lunch and pleasant afternoon with him and his German wife. The top-selling author showed me around the re-furbished old rectory, which had an indoor swimming-pool. He had a number of research-assistants and his study was packed with files. On the wall were clocks indicating all the time-zones of the world! I got the impression that Thomas lived his life halfway between the world of reality and that of imagination. But then that seems to be true of some celebrity creators of fiction.

The guest of honour in 1986 was Seán MacBride. For his work under the aegis of the UN for justice and peace in South-West Africa he had been awarded the Lenin Peace Prize and the Nobel Peace Prize. In his strange guttural accent he spoke about the danger of a nuclear holocaust, decried the arms race in which the two superpowers were engaged and urged writers, including members of P.E.N., to champion, and also be active in, peace and anti-nuclear-power movements.

In the following year Mrs Margaret Heckler, the new US ambassador, was the chief guest. She was jovial, outgoing and a fine speaker. A leading member of the Republican Party, she had had responsibility for education in President Ronald Reagan's first administration and was known to have been one of his close confidants.

As some politicians are prone to do, she spoke at some length. This was in sharp contrast to Francis Stuart, another special guest. He was not at all comfortable when addressing an audience and spoke very briefly. A very large person, and quietly-spoken, he did not even enjoy being in a crowd. However, he was most engaging when one talked to him face-to-face. This I had learned at University Church, when I prepared the papers for his third marriage after the death of his second wife. By a curious coincidence his first marriage in 1920 to Iseult, daughter of Maud Gonne, took place also in University Church. He told me it was a rather furtive ceremony, as at that time he was 'on the run' from the crown forces

Our principal speaker was Conor Brady, the distinguished journalist, who spoke about his profession. A newspaper, he said, could have a number of co-existing roles. It could aim at entertaining and bringing fun into the lives of its readers. Or, as he stated in words attributed to the legendary newspaperman, H.L. Mencken, it could set out to comfort the afflicted and afflict the comfortable. But for him the purpose of a good newspaper in society was twofold, namely, to allow that society to hold a mirror to itself and to give it a window on the wider world. These objectives, he insisted, were achieved by combining reporting which was factually based with commentary and analysis. The latter included subjective judgment which, he acknowledged, was not always proved to be sound. Conor did not conclude before raising a flag for his own newspaper, the *Irish Times*. He pointed out it had a long tradition of sending Irish journalists to report the wider world rather than simply relying on agency or wire reports, which inevitably were filtered through the eyes of British, US or European correspondents.

The British ambassador, Nicholas Fenn (later Sir Nicholas Fenn) and his wife, Susan, honoured the annual dinner in 1988. The actor, Alan Stanford, gave the best address I heard at any of our dinners. For me it was a most enjoyable occasion. Both the ambassador and his wife were born and raised in a manse, knew as much as I did about clerical life and were delightful company.

A year later I received a message from the British embassy enquiring if I would be free to accept an invitation to a dinner-party about a week later. I replied in the affirmative and was told it would be at Le Coq Hardi. As I had never heard of this restaurant, I had to check it out in the telephone directory. It was a family-run concern and when I arrived in the evening of the dinner I was warmly greeted by them. They were parishioners of Mount Merrion and knew me when I had served there.

It seems the dinner was in honour of a senior foreign office official, whose role was to visit (and, I suppose, inspect) embassies around the world. Apart from him the other guests were: Stephen Collins, the distinguished political journalist; Professor Ronan Fanning, history department, UCD; John FitzGerald, of the Economic and Social Research Institute; and Gerard Hogan, a lecturer in the law department, TCD. I was intrigued by the menu; the wine list was equally interesting. There were over a dozen dishes on offer. I noted the name of different kinds of food which I had not come across since reading Shakespeare's plays at college. The prices were extraordinary. I mumbled that they seemed to be excessive. Susan Fenn heard me and said in a tone heard by all: 'Fr Tony, don't be worried about the price. Just remember Margaret Thatcher is paying for all this'.

The man from the foreign office had a remarkable story to tell. He gave a riveting account of witnessing the fall of the Berlin Wall. A week earlier he happened to be in the British consulate in Berlin. On the late television news Berliners were to be seen pulling down parts of the Wall. This followed a confused statement, issued earlier, to the effect that the East German border police were not to be deployed to protect it. Like thousands of others, some in their night clothes, he went to witness for himself this historic event.

The official from the foreign office was very calm and self-assured. He was also pencil-thin and athletic-looking. I was not surprised by this feature. At this dinner in his honour, he ordered a large eating-apple and a small knife and spent the time slowly eating the apple, while the rest of us tucked into a Lucullan feast.

There was very little small talk at the dinner. The first topic of discussion was the prospect of the reunification of Germany. Helmut Kohl, the German chancellor, had developed a very positive relationship with Mikhail Gorbachev, leader of the Soviet Union, and did not find him unduly disposed to block German reunification. The other war allies: US, Great Britain and France were divided on the issue. The US and France were supportive of Kohl's determination to achieve German reunification as soon as possible. However, Prime minister Thatcher and her government were highlighting all kinds of reasons for delaying it, not least that the safety of Europe depended on a weak and divided Germany.

The British diplomats scarcely intervened in the general discussion. On the one hand, Stephen Collins and I argued that the best course of action was the rapid and peaceful reunification of Germany. This would eliminate further potential causes of conflict and would mercifully draw a line under the appalling events of the previous fifty years. On the other hand, the other guests approached the issue, it seemed to me, mainly from a British geopolitical perspective. I was also surprised at how cautious they were in expressing their opinions and their general deference. An attitude, I hasten to add, in no way encouraged by the ambassador.

Inevitably, the question of Northern Ireland arose. Here again Stephen Collins and I were at one, articulating an Irish nationalist point of view. The views of the others again seemed to me to have been heavily influenced by political correctness. Even the two-nations theory received an airing! I told the ambassador that as an Irish person I viewed Northern Ireland as Ireland's British problem not as Britain's Irish problem, that it was a political problem with religious overtones not a religious problem with political overtones and that the only lasting solution to the difficulties was British withdrawal after a long period of justice, peace and reconciliation. Collins' view, I hasten to add, was far more nuanced and less stark than mine.

In 1989 our guest of honour was Alice Taylor. Then at the peak of her popularity, in person and on the page she was redolent of what Daniel Corkery termed 'The Hidden Ireland'. David Marcus was the principal speaker. Irish P.E.N. was gratified in having an opportunity to acknowledge his sterling and selfless contribution to Irish writing and especially his encouragement of young aspiring writers, when he was literary editor of the Irish Press. I had my own reasons to be pleased. David, with a generous acknowledgement, had based *A land in flames* (1988), his third novel, on *Memoirs of Jeremiah Mee, RIC* and was a much cherished friend.

In the years that followed John Banville, Maeve Binchy, Ernest Bryll (Polish ambassador and poet), Mrs Jean Kennedy Smith (US ambassador) and John Wilson (a senior member of a number of Irish governments), among others, enhanced the annual dinner. Archbishop Robin Eames was the guest of honour in 1997, Niall Tóibín the principal speaker. Realising that the gathering was convivial rather than one at which serious matters were discussed the archbishop set aside his prepared script and gave as entertaining a stand-up, knock-about performance as I ever enjoyed. Niall Tóibín was close to confirming the received wisdom about the personality of the comic. He was silent and morose. However, when he got to his feet, he was also immensely entertaining with his own distinctive, laconic and dead-pan humour.

President Mary Robinson, the first woman to be president of Ireland, honoured the annual dinner in 1996. From the outset there was considerable emphasis on protocol and during the entire proceedings she did not seem to be relaxed. Much of her conversation with me was about the manner in which she was 'invigorating' the countryside by visiting and encouraging local communities, a role for which at that time she was receiving justifiable acclaim.

In her address she spoke about human rights and the plight of Ken Saro-Wiwa. He was at the centre of a struggle in the oil-rich province of Ogoni land in Nigeria, where people were attempting to defend their individual rights and their tribal rights against encroachment by multinational oil companies, backed by the federal military government. She did not, however, refer to what for me was the most important and basic right of all, the general right to life. Yet just over six months later she was appointed UN High Commissioner for Human Rights!

President Mary McAleese was the guest of honour in 1999 and 2001. There was a minimum of fuss about protocol and she manifestly enjoyed meeting as many people as she could. A person of high intelligence, she spoke interestingly and courageously on almost any topic. She and her husband, Martin, were excellent company and were rated by the committee the most popular guests at our annual dinner over many years.

I was delighted to have the opportunity to spend time talking to Mrs McAleese, about whom I had already formed a high opinion. I had met her in 1986 when she launched *The facilitators*. For the most part, this was an honest, courageous and well-argued account of how facilitators were being used consciously and unconsciously to promote the secularist agenda in all areas of life in Ireland. Her encouragement of the authors of the book ran counter to the prevailing ethos of the time. I met her again in 1996 when she chaired the inaugural lecture at the Eighth Desmond Greaves Summer School which is sponsored by the Irish Labour History Society. The topic was the then much-criticised 1937 Constitution. She recalled vividly her experience of seeing her home and those of Catholic neighbours in north Belfast being burnt by a hostile mob, with the tacit collusion of elements of the security forces. At such a time she pointed out one envied countries which had a written Constitution, guaranteeing the rights of every citizen.

It is sometimes stated that writers tend not to be sociable. I have never had evidence of this down through the years. I have found writers, almost without exception, and especially my colleagues in the

P.E.N. committee to be most congenial. And I recall with pleasure expatriates who from time to time served or are serving on the committee: Morgan Llewelyn (novelist); Anne McCaffrey (science fiction writer); O.Z.Whitehead (biographer) from the US; Pat Connole from Australia; Ian St James (novelist) from Britain; and Krzysztof Joseph and Maria Romanowski (translators) from Poland.

Ian St James was the pseudonym under which Don Taylor wrote. He had served in the British army and later resided as an expatriate writer in a number of 'Britain's trouble spots'. I suspected that his was a role in Ireland similar to that of John Betjeman (the future poet laureate) during World War II.

O.Z.Whitehead, member of the P.E.N. committee from 1983 until he died in 1998, was, perhaps, the most popular member to serve on it. Zebbie, as we called him, was born in New York in 1911. He had a passion for the theatre and delighted in acting professionally up to a few years before he died. He played secondary roles in a number of the most highly-acclaimed films produced at Hollywood and elsewhere in the 1930s,1940s, 1950s and 1960s. His most memorable role was as 'Al' in John Ford's 1940 film version of Steinbeck's *The Grapes of Wrath*. He knew many of the outstanding actors and actresses of that era and was a close friend of Lillian and Dorothy Gish, and Katherine Hepburn, about whom he enjoyed telling numerous anecdotes. Zebbie's other great passion was the Baha'i Faith, of which he became a member in 1950 and a leading personality from the 1960s onwards. Apart from an important memoir on Lillian Gish, his writing was on various aspects of the Baha'i Faith. His practice of his faith was edifying and in accordance with it he never lost an opportunity to champion and promote the highest standards and values in every area of personal and social behaviour.

People came to P.E.N. from widely different perspectives but all are at one in their lively and practical interest in the written word. To serve on the committee is to have the privilege of working with generous and talented persons.[1] I have down through the years been greatly enriched by their friendship.

1. For the Executive Committee of Irish P.E.N. 2001-2, see Appendix 3.

CHAPTER 10

Other literary associations

Through writing I have come into contact with a number of other interesting persons and societies. In researching the first and second editions of *Doneraile* and *Listowel and its vicinity* I became acquainted with Tom Armitage and Pádraig de Brún, who were mainly responsible for the successful establishment of the Kerry Archaeological and Historical Society.

A native of Templemore, Tom Armitage became Kerry County Librarian in 1961. With others, who had a practical interest in local history, he established the Kerry Archaeological and Historical Society in 1967. The object of the Society was 'the collection, recording, study and preservation of the history and antiquities of Kerry, including the preservation of historical and antiquarian remains and the promotion of scientific excavation'. This it was hoped would be achieved by a programme of lectures each year in the winter months, to which I have occasionally contributed, and outings to places of historical and archaeological interest in the summer months, as well as the annual publication of a journal. Tom was fortunate to have Pádraig de Brún, then a member of the staff in the Dublin Institute of Advanced Studies, edit the early issues of the journal. Thereby the quality of subsequent issues with regard to content and presentation was assured. The early issues were also enhanced by the cover designs of Seán O'Connor.

Tom was succeeded in 1971 by Mrs Kathleen Browne (*née* Turner). Under her watchful eye the various activities of the Society continued to flourish. She also prompted the Society to publish annually *The Kerry Magazine*. This contains articles of general interest on Kerry which have not reached the scholarly standards required for inclusion in the *Journal*.

To encourage local participation as well as interest, the ruling council of the Society was made up of eventually seven sub-committees. Each of these was charged with promoting activities in each of six districts in Kerry, and one had a similar responsibility with regard to a branch in Dublin. Each branch was headed by a vice president of the Society. From the outset Seán Ó Lúing, writer and historian, was responsible for the Dublin branch.

I had been an active member of the Society from 1968 onwards and when in 1976 invited to do so I agreed to head the Dublin branch. After succeeding Seán Ó Lúing I served until 1989. With my colleagues I oversaw a programme of lectures for members of the Society domiciled in Dublin. The lectures, some by members of the Dublin branch, were held in St Patrick's Training College, Drumcondra. One of the most memorable was by Mgr Frank Cremin on 'The nun of Kenmare'. Even after two hours he was as fresh as when he had begun and continued to hold the rapt attention of his listeners.

The first edition of *Doneraile* which I published in 1968 and the second revised edition in 1970 were well received locally. They included accounts of writers associated with the area. Donncha Ó Dúlaing, a native of the town and even then a well-known broadcaster, used the book extensively, especially the chapters on the writers, in his weekly popular radio programme.

In November 1968 Michael P. Linehan was prompted to publish in the *Irish Independent* a series of articles entitled 'A new look at Canon Sheehan of Doneraile'. Two years later, at the invitation of Robert F. Walker, I met him and Liam Brophy, who had also written on Sheehan, and others to formally establish 'The Friends of Canon Sheehan Society', later re-named 'The Canon Sheehan Literary Society'. Subsequently I became a member of this founding committee and agreed to be one of the new Society's patrons.

Lectures, readings and discussions were held each month in Buswell's Hotel. Apart from the first few years and subsequently, when controversial topics were discussed, these were not well attended. From the outset the Society promoted the writers' festival in Doneraile and some members of the group attended it each year. Notwithstanding the extraordinary commitment of the Society's chairman, Robert Walker, and its secretary, Mona O'Donnell, owing to a lack of support the Society was wound up in 1982.

In 1971 and 1972, apart from the renewed interest in Canon Patrick Sheehan and a growing awareness of the other writers associated with Doneraile, there was considerable coverage in the southern newspapers of Writers' Week, Listowel. At that time also Bord Fáilte was encouraging and helping communities to organise local festivals. As a result, a committee in Doneraile inaugurated a 'North Cork Writers' Festival' in October 1972.

Donncha Ó Dúlaing, on the invitation of the committee, agreed to be the director of the festival. It was decided to begin with a discussion of the novels of Canon Patrick Sheehan. John Jordan, from the English department in UCD, and Ben Kiely had published articles on Sheehan and were easily persuaded to lecture on different aspects of his writing. The committee invited me to speak at the formal opening of the festival. In addition, Donncha asked me to act as a 'minder' for the two Dublin *literati* during their time in Doneraile.

The festival was held over a weekend, with the formal opening on Friday evening, the Jordan and Kiely lectures on Saturday morning and outings in the afternoon to Edmund Spenser's Kilcolman Castle and the grave in Charleville of the poet, Seán Clárach Mac Domhnaill.

The opening ceremony was held in the parish hall. Lady Doneraile, Canon John Cotter, P.P., John Jordan, Ben Kiely and I sat on a long narrow stool on the stage. Donncha Ó Dúlaing was a local favourite son and obviously enjoyed his role as director. Although acting as MC, he spoke at greater length than the combined efforts of the rest of us on the stage. At that time the conflict in Northern Ireland was intense. In a number of references to it, Donncha did not hide his nationalist sentiments. I was conscious that Lady Doneraile, sitting next to me, was taken aback by some of his comments, and protesting groans from Jordan and Kiely were quite audible.

Following the opening there was liberal hospitality for the visitors, and Jordan and Kiely did not refuse any of it. It was well into the small hours when I managed to get them over to the Central Hotel (now the Mallow Park Hotel) where accommodation had been arranged for the three of us. With difficulty we gained admittance. At that time the Central Hotel was being extensively refurbished. The only accommodation available for us were small cubicles which had been partitioned off in a large meeting room. With the aid of the night porter I left Jordan and Kiely sitting on their beds.

For a long time I could not sleep as my companions stumbled in and out to the toilet. Eventually I fell into a deep sleep. About 4 a.m. I woke up in horror, conscious of a great weight having fallen on me and fearing that the ceiling had come down. As I became fully awake I found Ben Kiely, also shaking with fear, grappling with me. When he came to his senses he said: 'Christ, Father, thank God its you'.

I succeeded in delivering Jordan and Kiely for their lectures, one at 11, the other at 12.15. They performed creditably. It was surprised at how fresh and focused they were, considering their condition the previous evening. The lectures were held in the study hall of the Presentation Sisters secondary school. At the top of it was a more than life-size statue of Our Lady of Lourdes. Subsequently one report of the festival in the press was dominated by a picture of Ben Kiely lecturing with the large statue seemingly growing out of his right shoulder!

One of the outings on Saturday afternoon was to Kilcolman

Castle. Here Edmund Spenser wrote the English epic 'The Faerie Queen'. Donncha Ó Dúlaing gave an engaging presentation on Spenser and the history of the castle. Political antagonism and racial antipathy combined with religious hatred to blind Spenser to the Irish point of view. Donncha could not resist the opportunity provided by the occasion to make some pertinent remarks about current affairs. He detailed Spenser's infamous plan for the pacification of Ireland and suggested some parallels with the then current British policy in Northern Ireland. John Jordan was highly critical of these asides and made rather vitriolic remarks to anyone who was prepared to listen to him.

Another outing in the afternoon was a visit to Holy Cross cemetery, Charleville, to the grave of Seán Clárach Mac Domhnaill. Mainchín Seoighe, the historian, gave an interesting presentation on the poet. Mac Domhnaill (1691-1754) was a noted Gaelic poet, whose works included a translation of Homer. His farm, west of Charleville, was the meeting place of a 'Court of Poetry', frequented by such other well-known poets of the time as Liam Dall Ó hIfearnáin, Seán Ó Tuama and Aindrias Mac Craith ('An Mangaire Súgach).

After a few of Mac Domhnaill's poems had been read the party moved into a local public-house. In sharp contrast to Ben Kiely who the more he drank, the more amiable he became, John Jordan was affected otherwise and tended to become acrimonious. Within a half-an-hour he had seriously offended a number of local patrons of the public-house. With difficulty a few of us succeeded in rescuing him before he was harmed. Later that evening during a public debate on 'The nationalism of Canon Sheehan', which featured Kiely, Jordan and Ó Dúlaing, even the mild-mannered Kiely became quite emotional and aggressive. When, eventually, I had deposited my two charges on the Dublin train at Mallow I was quite relieved. That first North Cork writers festival received generous coverage in the media and, owing to the laudable efforts of the organising committee, the festival was to continue successfully until 1987.

In preparing books for publication during the last thirty five years I have conducted research in the archives and libraries of a variety of institutions at home and abroad. But I have done most of my reading in the National Library of Ireland and its adjunct, the Genealogical Office.

Founded under the Dublin Science and Art Museum Act 1877, the National Library was opened in 1890. By contrast the antecedent of the Genealogical Office, the Office of the Ulster King of Arms, was established much earlier. Its inception can be traced to 1552 during the reign of Edward VI. The Office of Arms became the Genealogical Office in 1943 when responsibility for it was transferred from the British to the Irish government. Edward MacLysaght was placed in charge of it as Chief Genealogical Officer. Soon afterwards this title was changed to that of Principal Herald. Eventually, however, MacLysaght opted for the title, Chief Herald of Ireland.

From the outset the National Library had exceptional directors. Among the best known were Richard Irvine Best (palaeographer and philologist), Robert Lloyd Praeger (botanist) and Richard James Hayes (linguist and bibliographer). The first director I had the pleasure of knowing was Patrick Henchy. Although universally popular, he was somewhat of a patrician. When he retired he took charge of the Chester Beatty Library.

Henchy was succeeded by Alf MacLochlainn. He was a writer of some consequence and was related to the Pearse brothers, Willie and Pádraig, who were leaders in the 1916 Rising. His term ended when he became chief librarian in UCG. He was followed by Michael Hewson, a long-serving member of the staff. However, he took early retirement and died not long afterwards at a relatively young age.

His successor, Patricia Donlon, was mainly responsible for the physical transformation of the Library. For decades, owing to its Cinderella status in the department of education, the funding for the Library bordered on the derisory. With the marked improvement in the economic condition of the country, she managed to persuade the authorities to make more realistic subventions to the Library. One result of her stewardship is that today the Library attracts visitors to view its splendid refurbishment. The present director, Brendan O'Donoghue, retired from the department of the environment, where he had served as secretary general, and took up his post as a new challenge. The most dynamic of the institution's directors to date, he has already enhanced the various activities, facilities and roles of the Library and initiated a number of new ones.

The staff of the National Library reminded me of an extended family and I became a friend of quite a number of them. I enjoyed occasionally meeting a few of the junior members – staunch 'Dubs' supporters – at Croke Park. Another friend was Edward MacLysaght. He was the outstanding 'character' associated with the National Library and the Genealogical Office. Even after he retired, he continued to haunt the premises, while researching his books on Irish families. Whenever he darted in or out of the reading room, he invariably came over to me for a chat.

One of these chats I did not enjoy. I was sitting in the front row of the reading room which was crowded, owing to the influx of the summer readers from the US and elsewhere. Mac, who was in his late eighties, wandered in. He faced me and in a very loud voice, as he was quite deaf at that time, told me that he had walked all the way in from his home in Blackrock. He had to do so, because the then almost annual bus-strike, coinciding with Horse-show week at Ballsbridge, was in progress.

Ignoring my efforts to have me join him outside, he continued to regale the reading room. He said that a week earlier he had been passing St Patrick's church in Monkstown. Remembering that later in the week he was to attend a grand-niece's wedding, he decided to go to Confession. He continued: 'I went into the box. The slide came over and there you were. It was too late to escape'. He gave a word for word account of our exchanges, the penance he received and his opinion of it. Then, suddenly realising that most of those in the reading room were sitting up listening to him, he said: 'Oh! my God', and retired. I was glad I had my back to the rest of those in the room.

Sir John Ainsworth was another member of the staff one noticed because he seemed to be so much out of his milieu. MacLysaght had hired him as his assistant in 1943. At that time Mac was an inspector for the Manuscripts Commission and was scouring the country for estate maps and papers. Cannily he judged that Ainsworth, by virtue of his social origins and English education, would be helpful in gaining access to the 'great houses' and persuading their owners to lodge their papers in the National Library. It was generally the afternoon when Ainsworth, a fine palaeographer, looking absent-minded, arrived in to spend a few hours cataloguing manuscripts. Occasionally he would be formally dressed in preparation for a dinner appointment later in the evening.

Ned Keane had also been brought into the Library by MacLysaght. Before the benefits of recent technology he completed the mammoth task of indexing *Griffith's Valuation, the Tithe Aplotment* books and the Land Commission records. His knowledge of local history and Irish land tenure in the nineteenth century was unrivalled, as was his readiness to share that knowledge.

If evidence was required that the staff were affected by events outside the Library, it was provided by Paul Keogh. A quiet and popular junior staff member, he was killed in a tragic road accident near the airport. At his obsequies it became known that he had been an active member of Sinn Féin.

Down the years the standard of service and friendliness has remained constant. In other areas, however, there have been changes, reflecting those outside the Library. The fabric of the building now reflects the general state of affluence. Since 1990 the practical implementation of the enlightened policy of ensuring equality of access to employment has seen more women at every staff level, including a nun in her religious attire. Over twenty years ago it was not unusual for one or two 'knights of the road' to check in to the Library during harsh weather to enjoy the heat and sleep face downwards on a desk. Such was the practical compassion and tolerance of staff and readers alike that no one would pretend to see them or even protest at their occasional loud snoring. Today such a situation is inconceivable. At that time also none of today's strict security arrangements were in place. All one had to do to use the reading room was to sign the entry book. To ensure that books were not pilfered or damaged the staff depended on the moral rather than legal and security imperative.

The reading room was a great leveller and imbued a spirit of cama-
raderie. It gave me the opportunity to become acquainted with some
of the country's leading writers and historians including Tim Pat
Coogan, Peter Costello, David Fitzpatrick, Peter Harbison, Charles
Lysaght, D.R. O'C. Lysaght, León Ó Broin, Maurice R. O'Connell,
Seán Ó Lúing, Pádraig Ó Snodaigh, Fintan O'Toole and Christopher
J. Woods. I found sharing information with fellow readers immensely
helpful and in this regard I was most indebted to Pádraig Ó Snodaigh.
It was also pleasant to renew the acquaintance of American academ-
ics who arrived each summer. Among these were: L. Perry Curtis,
James Donnelly, Robert Hogan and Arthur Mitchell, each a recog-
nised specialist in his own field of Irish studies.

In 1980 I was requested by Gerry Lyne and Dónal Ó Luanaigh to
become a member of the executive committee of the National
Library of Ireland Society. Conscious of my indebtedness to them and
their colleagues over the years, I readily agreed. The Society was
founded by Paddy Henchy in 1969. Its main aim was to provide a
wide band of support, in Ireland and overseas, for the National
Library. It was envisaged that this support would act as a lobby to persuade the authorities to increase the annual funding for the Library.

From the outset the Society organised for its membership, which
eventually rose to over 400, an annual series of lectures, readings and
films which featured some of the country's best-known film-makers,
writers and scholars. It also arranged outings to libraries, places of
archaeological and historical interest and heritage centres. And in
recent years it has published short works on the Library, its collection
and cognate subjects.

Much of the credit for the success of the Society must go to Dónal
Ó Luanagh and Gerry Lyne. The Society has not been without its difficulties. These arose mainly because some members of the executive
committee were not fully aware of or content with the Society's rather
restricted role. Then there was E. Maitland Woolf. He was an eccentric bookseller and a genuine and practical friend of the Library. 'A
barrack-room lawyer', from the time he joined the executive committee, he provoked far more discussion than the combined interven-

tions of all the other members. I was glad all these difficulties had been sorted out when I became chairman in 2000.

The founding members of the Society included Richael Ellman (biographer of Joyce), Patrick Lynch (the economist), Senator Michael Butler Yeats and Cearbhall Ó Dálaigh (later president of Ireland). They would be gratified at the manner in which the Society's main objectives are now being realised. This has been facilitated by the transfer in 1986 of responsibility for the Library from the department of education to the department of the Taoiseach and later to the department of Arts, Heritage, Gaeltacht and the Islands. A major building and development programme will see the addition of a refurbished old Kildare Street Club, and former College of Art to the Library complex. More significantly perhaps, with radically improved funding there has been a substantial increase in staff and the Library is now able to acquire many important literary and historical collections and valuable individual items which would otherwise have been lost to Ireland. Notwithstanding what the future may hold for the 'Celtic Tiger', these developments will ensure that the National Library will remain a significant centre for research and one of the nation's prized assets.

CHAPTER 11

Travel and Writing

I developed an enthusiasm for travel at a relatively early age. This was facilitated by membership of the 4th Kerry Troop of the Catholic Boy Scouts of Ireland. Michael Kennelly took charge of this troop in Listowel in 1941. His assistant scoutmaster was Tim Danaher who was succeeded by Niall Stack in 1948.

At our premises, made available by Niall Stack, the troop engaged in the usual scouting activities. Members were divided into patrols with their own leaders and dens. At the weekly meeting there was drilling and preparation for tests for merit badges: for cycling, first-aid, horse-riding, interpreter, woodwork, etc. An army instructor occasionally took us for gymnastics and exercises with Indian clubs. For a few years we were instructed in boxing and took part in a competition with members of other troops in the county. There were occasional Sunday hikes to the scenic spots on the river Feale.

When it came to our annual camp Michael Kennelly was at his most adventurous. While other troops did not venture beyond county boundaries, Michael took us further afield year after year. In 1944, when many of us had not reached our twelfth birthday, Michael took us for a week's stay in the An Óige hostel in Mountjoy Square in Dublin. A visit to *Irish Independent* house included a picture of the group on the roof which was published a few days later. There followed a climb to the top of Nelson's Pillar and visits to the Botanic Gardens, the Zoo and even a football match in Croke Park. In the hostel we had a sing-song with six or seven hikers from Shankill in Belfast. One of them was particularly entertaining and sang ballads about the linen mills and the shipyards. In 1945 we spent our summer camp partly in Dublin and partly in the An Óige hostel in Enniskerry. Apart from the beauty spots we visited in County Wicklow, my most abiding memory of it was the exhausting task we had in carrying in turn a large, black box, full of tinned food, on the long climb from the bus-stop in the village to the hostel.

In planning the annual camp for 1946 Michael was most imaginative. There was quite a lot of coverage in the press of an alleged apparition of Our Lady at Kerrytown, between Gweedore and Burtonport, in County Donegal. Michael managed to have us accommodated in the farmhouses of the Ward family and their neighbours who had reported the alleged apparition. On our way to Kerrytown we flew from Rineanna (now Shannon Airport) to Collinstown (now Dublin Airport) and later took the narrow-gauge railway from Letterkenny to Burtonport.

For our next camp Michael took us outside the country. Fr Leo Walsh, a friend from school days, invited Michael to join him and his troop from a parish in Leeds at their annual camp at Knaresborough, near Harrogate, in Yorkshire. As well as the scouts from Leeds, there was also a troop from Skipton at the camp. Apart from Fr Leo, all the English scout-leaders had seen active service in the British army and the camp was run along military lines. For us this was something of a novelty and we enjoyed it. This was not the case, however, with the English lads who had experienced it all before. The Leeds troop had a bugle and drum band. Peter O'Toole, who was very tall for his age, wearing a leopard-skin over his shoulders, was the big-drummer.

Peter, later to become the celebrated actor, was popular with his peers. Fr Leo, it seems, had been exceptionally kind and helpful to him in his early years and the two became close and life-long friends.

At that stage Michael Kennelly was informed that it was not the policy of the C.B.S.I. to organise annual camps outside the country, so he disaffiliated our troop from that organisation and we became the 1st Listowel Boy Scouts. Our summer camp that year, 1948, was at Gilwell Park, London, the headquarters of the Baden Powell Scouts. We benefited from a rigorous training in basic scouting and had an opportunity to visit the major sights of London and other places, such as Epping Forest. In that same year Michael and the troop organised a Jamborette in Listowel which was attended by over a hundred scouts from Britain and Europe.

For summer camp in 1949 we spent some days in Paris before travelling on to Lourdes. In Paris we were accommodated by Abbé Pierre Conan in his parish of St Severin. He and a troop of French Boy Scouts had been our guests in Listowel in the summers of 1946 and 1948. The parish hall, where we slept, and the rest of the parish plant bore signs of the neglect of the war years. About ten years later, when I visited Abbé Conan, the parish had been transformed. It had become one of the most prestigious and progressive parishes in the city and was popular with students and staff from the Sorbonne. My most abiding memory of our time in Lourdes was of a frightening thunder and lightning storm, the ferocity of which none of us had previously experienced, which suddenly broke out as we marched in full kit; rucksacks and sleeping-bags; and with the infamous black box to the railway station on our way home.

1950 was declared a Holy Year by Pius XII. After stop-overs at Aix-le-Bains and Zurich we travelled on to Rome. The Italian Federation of Boy Scouts had prepared a site, near the church of St Paul outside the walls, where scouts, arriving from all over the world, were able to camp. At that time the cold war between East and West was at its coldest. Between a third and a half of Italians were voting for the Communist Party and Italian governments were collapsing with alarming regularity. The heightened political temperature was almost palpable. In the areas surrounding the scout camp practically all the houses displayed large red flags with the hammer and sickle.

Joseph P. Walsh, the Irish minister to the Vatican, gave a reception for us. He also arranged that at a general papal audience Michael and his assistant scoutmaster, Niall Stack, and John Kennelly would personally hand a roll of Irish tweed to the pope for the poor children of Rome. We were accompanied to Rome by the Tuam troop of the C.B.S.I., one of whom was Tommy Murphy, the later playwright.

In 1951 a world scout jamboree was organised at Bad Ischl, near Salzburg. We travelled to it with the Tuam scouts. The jamboree had the appearance of a counter-rally, as at that time communist governments, regimes, and Parties were organising frequent enormous gatherings of communist youth movements and this was integrated into their general propaganda. Austria was occupied by the four major war allies: US, USSR, UK and France. Thus there was also an element of confrontation about the choice of the jamboree site. On the way to the jamboree our train was stopped and searched by US soldiers, while facing us a long train going in the opposite direction, packed with communist youth and bedecked with their flags, received similar treatment.

The jamboree was dominated by American scouts. There were representatives from many other countries but their numbers were not considerable. The US 8th army seemed to be everywhere helping their compatriots. There was incessant rain and the jamboree site practically became a sea of mud. After a few days some of us left to explore the scenic area around St Wolfgang.

Over the years Michael Kennelly had the troop put on concerts to subsidise our trips abroad. One of the most memorable was one in association with 'Rafaelle', the entertainer and alleged hypnotist. For weeks some of us practised pretending to be hypnotised and later acted as his assistants and props in his part of the show.

Apart from my early experience of foreign travel, my taste for it was further whetted by some remarkable travel writers. In the 1950s and 1960s John Gunther had few equals. His style was lively and his substantial volumes of six to seven hundred pages provided a fascinating overview of the super powers and whole continents. He devoted as much space to profiles of the governing elites of countries as to their history and geography. The style of Alan Moorehead was more restrained and subtle. But his accounts of his searches for the origins of the Blue and the White Niles or on the heroism and carnage at Gallipoli were no less engaging. And few could compare with Laurens van der Post writing on Africa. In recent years I found Bruce Chatwin, Paul Theroux and Dervla Murphy more successful than most in entertaining the armchair traveller. When researching local history I also discovered how valuable, as well as interesting, books by travellers can be. In *Listowel and its vicinity* I cited twenty-eight seventeenth, eighteenth and nineteenth-century travellers in Ireland.

For over forty years curiosity has prompted me to travel abroad once or twice a year to a different destination. I have led pilgrimages to the Holy Land, Rome and the various centres of Marian devotion in Europe and India, and attended Eucharistic Congresses at Munich, Melbourne and Philadelphia. For the most part I have gone abroad with a group or on a package holiday. These have had the added dimension, not least when originating from London, of giving me an opportunity to meet a wide variety of persons. On many occasions also I have holidayed on my own. On such trips I generally took along a book to read and review. It was on these trips that I also developed the practice of drafting articles on places I visited.

Following World War II communism was in the ascendant. One-third of the population of the world and one-third of the surface of the earth was controlled by adherents to communism. The bamboo and iron curtains ensured that the flow of information between the Western democracies and the communist world was kept to a minimum. In general, communist authorities allowed access to their countries only to members of communist Parties, or what the Western propaganda of the time called 'fellow-travellers' or again what Lenin in a memorable phrase described as 'useful idiots'. I was always eager to see for myself what conditions were like on the other side of these 'curtains' and I availed of every opportunity to do so.

In 1972 I visited the Soviet Union with a group of US and

Canadian tour operators who were exploring the possibility of organising tours there. For all of us the experience was quite a culture shock. With very few exceptions, no books, newspapers, periodicals, radio or TV, apart from those which promoted the administration or communist ideology, were tolerated. The limitations on communication and travel within the Soviet Union were extraordinary. Only apparatchiks had access to telephone directories. Nobody seemed to be able or willing to answer the most innocuous question. While we were in Russia an Aeroflot plane on a flight between Leningrad (now St Petersburg) and Moscow crashed with the loss of over a hundred passengers. No member of the general public in the Soviet Union ever heard of this. Knowledge of it surfaced in the West because seven members of the staff of the French embassy in Moscow lost their lives in the tragedy.

The shortage of all but the most basic food and the lack of quality in the clothing of people, except those who were members of the army or police, were striking. Overcrowded trams and the underground, in Moscow, were the sole means of transport. There were no cars, motorbikes or even bicycles. Great crowds of people were continually on the move on foot in the streets.

After the communist revolution places of worship were closed down. Two churches on the edge of Red Square had been turned into museums: one depicting the history of the Communist Party, the other the life and achievements of Comrade Lenin. We were even taken to visit a shop promoting atheism!

Some years earlier General Charles de Gaulle, then president of France, had visited Moscow. He had indicated that while there he wished to assist at Mass on Sunday. To facilitate him the authorities re-opened the Church of St Louis of France, near Red Square. When in Moscow I managed to find it and celebrated Mass there. The handful of octogenarians and the Polish priest I met informed me that the church was under continual surveillance. The atmosphere in Leningrad, with its fabulous art treasures, was just as Orwellian as in Moscow; two other destinations Sochi on the Black Sea and Tbilisi in Georgia less so. A feature of Tbilisi was the extraordinary number of men to be seen in various stages of drunkenness in public places.

In 1978 I joined a tour which travelled through East Germany, Czechoslovakia and Hungary. They had all the features of communist administered countries, not least the obvious lack of maintenance of buildings and infrastructure, and a general shabbiness. In Berlin the wall dividing the city and the East from the West was a monument to the failure of the communist system. The authorities had to build it to prevent their citizens from fleeing in their tens of thousands to the West. On one side of the wall, West Berlin was even more affluent in appearance and brash than a downtown area in any US metropolis. On the other, East Berlin had its pre-war appearance with many of its poorly restored buildings still showing signs of the intensive fire-fights which took place there in the last stages of the war. At 'Check Point Charlie', where we crossed from West to East Berlin, tanks belonging to NATO and the Warsaw Pact symbolically faced each other. While humour was in short supply in East Berlin, this was not so in West Berlin. In one of his many asides the city guide pointed to a statue of a horse in full flight with a naked rider and told us that it was a monument to the last tax-payer fleeing from Berlin.

In 1981 I joined ten others on a guided tour of six cities in China: Hong Kong, Canton, Hangshow, Shanghai, Nanking and Peking. Hong Kong was what I expected it to be: a human ant-hill. The manner in which the five million people on a small island and some adjoining territories so successfully ordered their lives and habitat was admirable.

The People's Republic of China was entirely different. Its citizens were still slowly recovering from the harrowing decade between 1966 and 1976. During that period, with the collusion of Mao Tse-Tung, the Red Guards had charged around the country, promoting the Cultural Revolution. One result of this campaign was the 'elimination' of about one million people. For the Red Guards involvement in education was a sign that a person was a member of the bourgeoisie, so hundreds of thousands of professors, teachers and others, who had a third or even a second level education, were banished to the paddy fields, whence many were never to return alive. One of the most idiotic impulses released by slogans of the 'Little Red Book' was a determination to kill small birds on the assumption that they were as destructive as rodents. So successful were the Red Guards in their endeavours to this end, that I and my fellow-tourists were conscious of an eerie silence in the countryside and parks we visited.

The wife of Mao Tse-Tung and the other members of the 'Gang of Four' had attempted to continue his brutal regime. They were ousted and put on trial. The nonplussed Chinese were treated to hours of the trial on State TV. The Chinese media carried no reports sourced outside the country. So seldom, if ever, did the Chinese see a picture of a non-Chinese person that whenever we alighted from our minibus a rather intimidating crowd of over a hundred would gather round to stare in silence at us. At that time, apart from the omnipresent military, who wore bright green uniforms, with red flashes, practically every living Chinese, man or woman, old or young, was dressed exactly alike in the faded-blue tunic, trousers and cap of Chairman Mao. It seems that until a short time before our visit any variation from the 'revolutionary dress' was not allowed.

All religions were suppressed in the People's Republic. The Christian Churches were harshly dealt with, particularly the Catholic Church because of its international connections. In Hong Kong I was briefed on the situation and agreed to deliver a message to a Jesuit in Shanghai. I met him in a hotel room and he left me in no doubt how hazardous it was for Chinese Catholics at that time to practise their Faith.

In the People's Republic the imperative for total uniformity was draconian. A wide range of 'anti-social behaviour' was punished by a peremptory death sentence. Thus local guides were able to tell us that there was no crime!

A considerable part of China is mountainous and non-arable. At that time it was inhabited by a billion people, about one quarter of the earth's population. When faced with these realities, I found it difficult to counter the argument that the discipline required to regiment such an enormous and dense population could be provided only by an authoritarian administration.

In 1983 a group of Irish trade-unionists, officials and members, chartered a plane for a trip to Cuba. As some seats were left unoccupied, their agent, Shamrock Travel, advertised them. Despite a last-minute attempt by the organisers to prevent me from travelling, I was able to insist on going, as I had already paid my fare.

Soon after we arrived in Havana it was clear that most of my travelling companions were determined to be favourably impressed by whatever they were to see or hear. The Cuban revolution had much to recommend it. The widespread corruption characteristic of previous administrations had been swept away, as had the unacceptable domination by the US of the commercial and political life of Cuba. The Cuban revolutionaries had also vastly improved education and medical services and, most importantly, made them equally accessible to all. But a heavy price had to be paid for these significant improvements. As in other communist countries, the poor state of buildings and infrastructure was quite noticeable. Apart from basic items of food, which was subject to rationing, there were serious shortages of all other consumer goods, this for the most part caused by the embargo enforced by the US on Cuba. The greatest disadvantage, however, was the effective abolition of democratic freedoms by a one Party State. This was achieved mostly by the oppressive activities of local, neighbour-watch style communist committees which ensured that there was no organised opposition nor even political dissent of any kind.

I was fascinated by the meetings the group had with representatives of the Communist Party in Cuba, the Federation of Cuban Women, the Young Communist League and a few Workers' Councils. The meetings were followed by carefully supervised question and answer sessions. At these the command economy and the central control of seemingly everything else were described and lauded. At a meeting with members of the Cuban Trade Union Movement we learned that, while 17 per cent of trade unionists were members of the Communist Party and 13 per cent belonged to the Young Communist League, the allegation that the trade union movement in Cuba was an appendage of the Party was a capitalist lie! We also learned that there were no strikes in Cuba, as they were against the law and that, in any case, they were counter-revolutionary being directed against the workers themselves who were ruling the country.

On my first Saturday in Havana I visited the cathedral, where next door I met a Jesuit, with whom I later concelebrated Mass. He told me that the auxiliary bishop of Havana would be celebrating Mass on Sunday morning at 10.30. I joined the bishop. Mass was in a small side-chapel as the rest of the building was in an advanced state of disrepair. About thirty elderly people attended. As on the previous evening two plain-clothes policemen came in as Mass began, obtrusively noticed those who were present and then switched on loudspeakers outside. The martial music was so loud that the bishop and I could scarcely hear our own voices.

At Varadero, a resort area with a long beach, on which no one was to be seen, the group spent four days. From the hotel I noticed a small church some miles distant on the edge of the beach. After passing through a cordon manned by militia around the hotel, I eventually reached it. I met a priest in the tiny sacristy which served as his bedsit. He was a Canadian from one of the maritime provinces and he had a remarkable story to tell. It seems, as part of the repression of the Catholic Church, the Cuban Revolutionary Council ordered all non-Cuban priests and religious to leave the country. This resulted in the reduction of between a third and a quarter of the Church's personnel. At that time, with one exception, only governments of communist and non-aligned countries had diplomatic relations with Cuba. The Federal Government of Canada was that exception. The Cuban bishops appealed to their Canadian counterparts for as many replacements as possible for the expelled priests. Two dozen Canadian priests answered the appeal. However, when they had spent a year in Cuba the ruling Revolutionary Council decided they were a threat to the 'security of the nation' and expelled them. On learning this, Pierre Trudeau, the Canadian prime minister, communicated with Fidel Castro and had them all back within a week!

Later that evening I accompanied the Canadian in his twenty-year-old, battered Volkswagen to a distant village to celebrate Mass. About thirty people of all ages attended. After Mass we were invited by one family to a meal. The fare on offer and the decrepit state of the village and its little chapel left me in no doubt as to the grinding poverty of these people. In his area, where he was responsible for seven parishes, the Canadian informed me that conditions were relatively tolerable. In other areas, however, it seems priests were even prevented from conducting Christian burials for deceased parishioners. Subsequently, as a result of my first-hand experience of Cuba, I was prompted to challenge in the *Sunday Independent* and the *Furrow* misleading reports by other Irish visitors to the island about that time.

During trips to Bulgaria, Poland and Romania in 1982, 1986 and 1988 respectively I witnessed the extent to which the communist system had failed these countries. The social and political conditions in Romania were extraordinary. Few, if any, goods in the shops, long lines of people waiting for food deliveries, no electric power after 6 p.m.; this side by side with monumental building projects in the centre of Bucharest to glorify Nicolae Ceaucescu and his regime.

In October 1996 I witnessed some of the appalling consequences following the nemesis of former Yugoslavia. Fr Kevin Doheny, CSSp, invited me to accompany him on a tour of projects established by Refugee Trust in that war-devestated area. With Fr Norman Fitzgerald, CSSp, he had founded this organisation after being involved in working for refugees in Biafra during the Nigerian civil war.

His colleague, Brother Thomas O'Grady, OH, drove us through Bosnia to Sarajevo. On long stretches of the road only the charred remains of buildings were to be seen. Much of Sarajevo was like Berlin, and Dresden after World War II. Yet people were courageously attempting to return to normal life. We visited a number of community centres which provided day-care services for Croats, Serbs and Muslims alike on both sides of the peace line, and a hospital, supported by the Irish government, on the outskirts of Sarajevo. At Mostar the Trust had a community centre which again, on both sides of the peace line, was attempting to cope with the problem of accommodating thousands of refugees.

Apart from my eagerness to view the conditions prevailing in communist countries, I have had a fascination with exotic destinations in Africa, Asia and especially South America. I had always enjoyed reading about them. But, as the Chinese proverb says, 'To see once is better than to hear a thousand times'. Hence my enthusiasm over the years to see them for myself. Not least to share the joys of travel, I have occasionally written about places I found particularly interesting. However, notwithstanding my wanderlust and the attractiveness of near and faraway places, I have never returned home without realising how fortunate I am to have been born and to be residing in Ireland.

Report on 66th World Congress of P.E.N. International

The 66th World Congress was held in the University of Warsaw in June 1999. Delegates from more than 70 countries attended. With Krzysztof Joseph and Maria Romanowski, two other members of our executive committee, I represented Irish P.E.N.

The theme of the Congress was 'Farewell to the 20th Century'. The unparalleled scientific and technological progress achieved throughout the century, the fall of empires, the end of colonialism, clear gains for women's rights and people becoming more equal – all tend to be over-looked when one reflects on the horrors associated with the century. One need but recall the slaughter in World War I, the Gulags, the Holocaust, the nuclear torching of the populations of Hiroshima and Nagasaki and the ethnic cleansing in Rwanda and the Balkan conflicts. In Warsaw, razed to the ground in November 1944 at the whim of a maniac, and in Poland, over which the greatest wars of the recent past raged and where the Holocaust was perpetrated by the Nazis, one could not but be acutely aware of those horrors. Few of those who contributed to the various discussions failed to refer to these unhappy aspects of the 20th century. Great stress was laid on the challenge to writers to ensure that in these instances at least history did not repeat itself.

Other challenges set out for the writer on the threshold of the 21st century and the new millennium were the need to encourage people to oppose totalitarianism and dictatorship and to caution people against the danger of abandoning a sense of community and becoming mere lonely inhabitants in the global village. The need for man to respect nature was highlighted as was the importance of ensuring that science was the servant of man not man the servant of science.

Somewhat idealistically it was proposed that the manner in which writers could successfully face such challenges was by the unqualified pursuit of truth. This seeking of truth, it was stressed, was not to be deflected by ideological agendas. Nor was it to be frustrated by censorship.

Another issue which attracted the attention of congress was the dumbing-down of culture in general and literature in particular by present-day commercialism. In a paper on the subject Ronald Harwood of English P.E.N. acknowledged the manner in which technology and the media had facilitated unprecedented access to cultural activities of all kinds. However, he detailed how the pressure of the market-place caused publishers and editors to ignore literature of the highest quality and to promote the banal and the kitsch. He urged writers to challenge this development but was not able to offer any specific advice on how the trend could be reversed.

Other important meetings were included under the umbrella of congress such as those convened by a Writers for Peace Committee and Women's Writers Committee. Strong support was given to a Universal Declaration of Linguistic Rights by the Translation and Linguistic Rights Committee. At congress there was a seminar organised by UNESCO on 'The Role of International Writers' Organisations' in the 20th Century and their association with UNESCO'.

Writers in prison were not forgotten. At a press conference a detailed case-list of fellow-writers in prison, those who had been tortured and those who had been murdered was provided. For the most part they were citizens of the remaining Communist controlled countries: China, Cuba, North Korea, Vietnam and Yugoslavia. But other countries such as Iran, Iraq, Mexico, Myanmar (Burma) and Turkey also had their complement of prisoners of conscience!

The congress at plenary and subordinate sessions emphasised the importance it attached to this aspect of P.E.N.'s activities. Professor Doan Viet Hoat of the Buddhist University of Ho Chi Minh city, who was released in September 1998 mid-way through an 18-year prison sentence, largely owing to lobbying by Polish P.E.N., was the chief guest of honour at congress. And a monograph circulated to those attending the congress indicated how dangerous it can be in some parts of the world to speak or write the truth. It carried on its front cover an appreciation of Slavco Curuvija, editor of several independent newspapers, and a detailed account of the background to his assassination in Belgrade on 11 April 1999.

Rules of Irish P.E.N.

NAME AND OBJECTS OF P.E.N.

1. The association shall be called P.E.N. (i.e. Poets, Playwrights, Editors, Essayists, Novelists). Translators shall be eligible as members. The Association exists to promote the friendly co-operation of writers in every country in the interests of literature, freedom of expression and international goodwill.

QUALIFICATION FOR MEMBERSHIP

2. The qualification for membership shall be recognized standing in the literary world. The committee shall be the final judge of the qualification of any candidate for election. Members shall be required to subscribe to the principles laid down in the P.E.N. charter, as passed at the international congress held in Copenhagen in 1948, viz:

P.E.N. affirms that:

(1) Literature, national though it be in origin, knows no frontiers, and should remain common currency between nations in spite of political or international upheavals.

(2) In all circumstances, and particularly in time of war, works of art, the patrimony of humanity at large, should be left untouched by national or political passion.

(3) Members of P.E.N. should at all times use what influence they have in favour of good understanding and mutual respect between nations; they pledge themselves to do their utmost to dispel race, class and national hatreds and to champion the ideal of one humanity living in peace in one world.

(4) P.E.N. stands for the principle of unhampered transmission of thought within each nation and between all nations, and members pledge themselves to oppose any form of suppression of freedom of

expression in the country and community to which they belong. P.E.N. declares for a free press and opposes arbitrary censorship in time of peace. It believes that the necessary advance of the world towards a more highly organised political and economic order renders a free criticism of governments, administrations and institutions imperative. And since freedom implies voluntary restraint, members pledge themselves to oppose such evils of a free press as mendacious publication, deliberate falsehood and distortion of facts for political and personal ends.

Membership of P.E.N. is open to all qualified writers, editors and translators who subscribe to these aims, without regard to nationality, race, colour or religion.

SUBSCRIPTIONS

3.   Members shall pay such subscription as shall be decided at an annual general meeting.

Payment of Subscriptions

4.   The annual subscription shall become due on the 1st January in each year or on any other date which shall be determined from time to time.

ELECTION OF MEMBERS

5 (a) The name, permanent address and qualifications of every candidate for membership shall be entered on the application form.

The candidate must be proposed and seconded by two members of the Centre tm both of whom, preferably, he or she should be personally known and both of whom should be familiar with his or her works; both these sponsors must sign the application form and shall – if required by the committee – produce evidence in writing of qualifications.

Every candidate shall be elected by a majority vote at a committee meeting and the decision of such majority shall be final. A candidate having failed to secure election at a committee meeting shall not be eligible to be proposed for election again until the expiration of six months.

(b) Temporary membership may be granted to visiting writers, editors or translators from other countries during the period of their residence in this country.

HONORARY MEMBERS

6. The committee may invite to be members of honour such persons as they shall think fit.

COMMITTEE – NUMBER AND CONSTITUTION

7. The management of the Centre is vested in a committee consisting of the chairman, the vice-chairman, the honorary secretary and the honorary treasurer (who shall be ex-officio members), and such other members of the Centre as the committee may decide.

    Five members of the committee shall form a quorum. The committee shall have power to fill any vacancies in their number.

ELECTION OF COMMITTEE

8 (a) Four members of the outgoing committee shall be elected by the committee prior to the annual general meeting, to serve on the incoming committee.

 (b) The officers and remaining members of the committee shall be elected at the annual general meeting.

CASTING VOTE

9. In all cases of the committee coming to a division, if the numbers be equal, the chairman, in addition to his vote as a member of the committee shall have a casting vote.

SUB-COMMITTEES

10. The committee shall have power to elect sub-committees.

ANNUAL GENERAL MEETING

11. The date of the annual general meeting and of any other meetings shall be fixed by the committee.

Report at Annual General Meeting

12. An abstract of the audited accounts for the past year shall be available at the annual general meeting.

ALTERATION OF RULES

13. At the annual general meeting any motion for the alteration of the rules or otherwise affecting the interests of P.E.N. may be brought forward by any member; but no such motion shall be made unless seven days' notice has been given by sending a copy of the motion to the honorary secretary.

LIABILITY OF MEMBERS

14. The liability of the committee and members shall be limited to the amount of their subscriptions, and any rights which a member may have in P.E.N. shall be determined to have ended when his membership ceases.

MEMBERSHIP

15. Membership of one Centre constitutes membership of all.

ASSOCIATE MEMBERS

16. The committee may elect associate members.

Consultative Council of Irish P.E.N.. The Consultative Council of Irish P.E.N. was formed in 1954 at the unanimous wish of both the Belfast and Dublin Centres. The Council consists of four members from the Belfast Centre and four members from the Dublin Centre as appointed by the committee of each Centre. The Council meets at intervals in either Belfast or Dublin to discuss matters of mutual interest or matters on which joint action is deemed desirable and to elect annually a president of Irish P.E.N.

Executive Committee of Irish P.E.N.
2001-2

President: John B. Keane (writer and playwright)

Life Member: Séamus Heaney (poet and Nobel laureate)

Chairman: Very Reverend Dr J. Anthony Gaughan (writer and historian)

Secretary: Arthur Flynn (writer)

Treasurer: Mrs Nesta Tuomey (novelist)

Members: Mrs Marita Conlon McKenna (novelist)
                     Mrs Christine Dwyer Hickey (novelist)
                     Mrs Sheila Flitton (actress and novelist)
                     James Maher (biographer)
                     Mrs Patricia O'Reilly (writer and novelist)
                     Krzysztof Joseph Romanowski (translator)
                     Dr Maria Romanowski (translator)
                     Mrs Kathleen Sheehan O'Connor (novelist)

Writings

A
BOOKS AND BOOKLET

1969   *The concept of being: A study in metaphysics.*

1970   *Doneraile.*

1972   *The Synan family.*

1973   *Listowel and its vicinity .*

1975   *Memoirs of Constable Jeremiah Mee, R.I.C.*

1977   *Austin Stack: Portrait of a separatist.*

1978   *The Knights of Glin.*

1979   (Joint ed.) *St Michael's College, Listowel.*

1980   *Thomas Johnson (1872-1963) : First Leader of the Labour Party in Dáil Éireann.*

1981   (Booklet, ed.) *Mount Merrion, the old and the new.*

1983   *A political odyssey: Thomas O'Donnell (M.P. for West Kerry 1900-1918).*

1984   *Travels on four continents.*

1985   (Ed.) [Alfred O'Rahilly's] *The crucified.*

1986   *Alfred O'Rahilly I: Academic.*

1989   *Alfred O'Rahilly II: Public Figure.*

1992   *Alfred O'Rahilly III: Controversialist, Part I Social Reformer.*

1993   *Alfred O'Rahilly III: Controversialist, Part 2, Catholic Apologist.*

1995   *Olivia Mary Taaffe (1832-1918): Foundress of St Joseph's Young Priests Society.*

1996   (Ed.) *Memoirs of Senator Joseph Connolly: A Founder of Modern Ireland.*

1997   *Newman's University Church: A History and Guide.*

1998   (Ed.) *Memoirs of Senator James G. Douglas: Concerned Citizen.*

2000   *At the coal face: recollections of a city and country priest: 1950-2000.*

B
ARTICLES AND OBITUARIES

1974   'Vocations', *Intercom*, November.

1976   'There's room at our inn – a Dublin contribution', *Intercom*, December.

1978   'Over mud roads to Mass centre', *Irish Independent* 21 March.

       'Listowel and the Fleadh Cheóil', *Clár Cuimheacháin Fleadh Cheóil na hÉireann, Lios Tuathail.*

       'Listowel hosts Fleadh Cheóil, *Irish Independent* 22 August.

       'The wall that cuts a capital city in two', *Irish Independent* 4 November.

'Madness and murder in the Vienna woods', *Irish Independent* 7 November.

'Hungary: tip-toeing towards freedom?', *Irish Independent* 21 November.

1979 'The fever hospital that became a noted college', *Irish Independent* 2 June.

'A scoop that never was', *Irish Times* 12 December.

1980 'Where Irishmen fell fighting at the Alamo', *Irish Independent* 1 February.

'Dallas - where a dream died', *Irish Independent* 5 February.

'Houston means more than "mission control"', *Irish Independent* 8 February.

'Tame Indians and dude cowboys', *Irish Independent* 12 February.

'Doing a Jinks', *Irish Times* 4 March.

'A memorable lesson for Belfast employers', *Irish Times* 12 August.

1981 'An enterprise to be proud of', *Leinster Leader: Centenary Supplement* 15 November.

'Austin Stack: an assessment', *Kerrymen 1881-1981* (ed., John P. McCarthy).

'Death of Captain Thomas Shanahan [obituary]', *Kerryman* 1 May.

'The field that I knew so well', *Lios Tuathail: Páirc Mhic Shíthigh* (ed., John Molyneaux) Bealtaine.

'Counting house of the Orient', *Irish Times* 19 August.

'City of milling crowds, *Irish Times* 20 August.

'After the revolution', *Irish Times* 24 August.

'Don't open the window when typhoon comes', *Irish Times* 25 August.

'Ancient capital', *Irish Times* 26 August.

'Contrasting walls of China', *Irish Times* 27 August.

'Football memory', *Kerryman* 2 October.

1982 'Fire-dancing and empty churches', *Irish Times* 26 July.

'A forest of standing stones', *Irish Times* 27 July.

'Homilies for October', The *Furrow*, September.

1983 Foreword in Patrick F. Meehan, *The members of parliament for Laois and Offaly (Queen's and King's Counties) 1801-1918* (Portlaoise).

'A trade-union visit to Cuba (1): They didn't want to talk about "Solidarity"', *Evening Echo* 10 March.

'A trade-union visit to Cuba (2): Classroom was usual Castroite battle-ground', *Evening Echo* 11 March.

'The gold of El Dorado', *Irish Times* 24 December.

1984 'City dominated by its recent past', *Limerick Association Yearbook 1984*.

'The Dialogue Mass', *The Furrow*, May.

'Wonders of South America (1): Many injustices live on in South

America', *Evening Echo* 22 May.

'Wonders of South America (2): Hazard of floods along lofty mountainsides', *Evening Echo* 23 May.

'Wonders of South America (3): Many symbols of Buenos Aires' tortured history', *Evening Echo* 29 May.

1985   'Archbishop Dermot Ryan 1924-1985 [obituary]: We will recall most his dedication', *Evening Herald* 22 February.

'Introduction - Céad Míle Fáilte Romhaibh', *Brochure: Writers' Week*.

'Fidel Castro's Cuba', *The Furrow*, August.

'Alfred O'Rahilly's The Crucified', The *Furrow*, December.

1987   'Sri Lankan journey', *Limerick Association Yearbook*.

'Tamils fail to muster enough strength to negotiate', *Irish Times* 25 April.

'Reply to Angela McNamara', *Reality*, October.

'His idea was to build a barn', *Irish Catholic* 1 October.

'There's nothing finer than Finland', *Sunday Press* 4 October.

'Patrick O'Brien [obituary]', *Kerryman* 20 November, *Irish Times* 3 December.

'The Irish work ethic', *The Furrow*, December.

'Father Robert Walsh [obituary]', *Kerryman* 11 December.

1988   'Our Lady, Seat of Wisdom', A walking tour of Dublin churches.

'Newman's church in Dublin', *News and Views* (TCD chaplaincy) 4 January

'The shot that killed Michael Collins', *Irish Times* 20 August.

'Martinique - an island paradise', *Sunday Press* 11 September.

'Saint Laurence O'Toole 1128-1180', *The Sacred Heart Messenger*, November (written at request of Archbishop Desmond Connell and published over his name).

1989   'Clonliffe and the revenue police', *Irish Catholic* 20 July.

'Father Fionán O'Sharkey (1919-1988) [obituary]', *Friends of Cardinal Newman: Newsletter*, autumn.

1990   'Reflections arising from the Dublin Diocesan Renewal Programme', *Link-Up*, July.

'The Dublin Diocesan Renewal Programme', *The Furrow*, July-August.

1991   'The late Michael Mulvihill', *Kerryman* 5 April. 'Michael Mulvihill [obituary]', *Irish Times* 10 May.

'Twenty-one years agrowing', *Kerryman* 24 May.

1992   'Morality and work', *Intercom*, October. Reprinted in Reality, January 1993.

'Sicily, idyllic tourist destination', *Sunday Press* 18 October.

1994   'Mission fields', *Irish Catholic* 2 June.

'Rite and reason: high pay for executives is leading to fewer jobs', *Irish*

Times 18 October.

1995 'The late Michael Kennelly - Listowel's Everyman', *Kerryman* 19 May.

'Hard to beat the warmth of Filipinos', *Irish Catholic* 22 June.

1996 'Remembering the "Old Faith"', *Intercom*, November.

1997 'Newman's University Church', *Intercom*, March.

'Easter Week 1916', *Kerry Magazine*.

'Clergy formation: self-formation', *Intercom*, May.

'The Catholic Church in the Ukraine', *Intercom*, November.

1998 'The RIC man who became a bishop', *Irish Catholic* 10 September.

'Very Reverend Patrick Murray (1911-1998) [obituary]', *Link-Up*, October/November.

1999 'Ghana's Church', Outlook: Holy Ghost Mission Bulletin, April-May.

'A chapel fit for a king', *Irish Catholic* 1 April.

'John Mary Pius Boland (1870-1958)', 'Joseph Connolly (1885-1961)', 'James G. Douglas (1887-1953)', 'Thomas Johnson (1872-1963)', 'Jeremiahh Mee (1889-1953)', 'Thomas O'Donnell (1871-1943)', 'Austin Stack (1889-1953)', 'Olivia Mary Taaffe (1832-1918)', *Dictionary of Irish biography*, forthcoming [2005].

'New Poland', *Irish Catholic* 24 June.

'The Listowel police meeting 70 years ago', *Kerryman* 2 July.

2000 'Retracing footsteps of St Columbanus', *Irish News* 28 October; 'Honouring St Columbanus', *Intercom*, November.

2001 'Thoughts for today' [Sermon notes for Sundays in February], *Intercom*, February.

'The wonders of India's many Christian shrines', *Irish News* 1 February, 'Ecumenism is a live force in India' *Intercom*, April.

'Island places safety in the hands of the Almighty', *Irish News* 29 March.

'A priest for war and peace', *Irish News* 12 July.

'Celebrating our cherished Christian link with Germany', *Irish News* 16 August.

'At the heart of Europe', *Irish News* 15 November.

'A writer by accident', *50 years a-growing: the history of the Kerry Association in Dublin* (ed. Mary McAuliffe).

2002 'The great vocation', *Irish News* 25 April.

'A modern pilgrims progress', *Irish News* 6 June.

C

BOOK REVIEWS

1975 Patrick Corcoran (ed.), *Looking at 'Lonergan's Method'*, The Bulletin: *Dublin diocesan pastoral review*, Aug-Sept.

1976 Emmet Larkin, *The Roman Catholic Church and the creation of the modern*

Irish state 1878-1886, Evening Herald 29 April.

1981 Marina Warner, *Joan of Arc. The image of female heroism, Sunday Press* 30 August.

1982 John J Dunne, *The pioneers, Sunday Press* 7 February.

1985 Michael J. Walsh (ed.), *Butler's lives of the saints: concise edition, Irish Press* 23 February.

1986 David Yallop, *In God's name, an investigation into the murder of Pope John Paul I, Limerick Association Yearbook.*

Patrick J. Corish, *The Irish Catholic experience: a historical survey, Irish Press* 11 January.

Nessan Shaw, OFM (ed.), *The Irish Capuchins (record of a century 1885-1985), Irish Press* 19 April.

León Ó Broin, *Just like yesterday, Studies,* autumn.

Doris Manly, Loretto Browne, Valerie Cox and Nicholas Lowry, *The facilitators, Intercom,* September.

1987 Patrick O'Farrell, *The Irish in Australia, Kerryman* 4 September.

F. M. Carroll (ed.), *The American Commission on Irish Independence 1919: the diary, correspondence and report, Studies,* winter.

1988 Trevor West, *Horace Plunkett: co-operation and politics, an Irish biography, Studies,* spring.

D. G. Boyce (ed.), *The revolution in Ireland 1879-1923, Sunday Press* 1 May.

Hubert Butler, *The children of Drancy, Sunday Press* 2 October.

Delia Smith, *A Journey into God, Sunday Press* 27 November.

S. P. Farragher, CSSp, *Père Leman (1826-1880), Sunday Press* 4 December.

1989 Robert Morley, *The pleasures of age, Limerick Association Annual.*

R. F. Foster, *Modern Ireland 1600-1972, Studies,* spring.

Catherine B. Shannon, *Arthur J. Balfour and Ireland 1874-1922, Studies,* autumn.

Thurston Clarke, *Equator - a journey around the world, Sunday Press* 10 September.

1991 Norman Vance, *Irish literature: a social history, Studies,* spring.

Michael D'Antonio, *Fall from grace, Sunday Press* 24 March.

John P. Duggan, *A history of the Irish army, Studies,* winter.

K. Woodward, *Making saints, Irish Catholic* 21 November.

1992 Dan van der Vat, *Freedom was never like this: a winter's journey in East Germany, Sunday Press.* 26 January.

Gerald McElroy, *The Catholic Church and the Northern Ireland crisis 1968-86, Studies,* autumn.

William Martin, *The Billy Graham story: a prophet with honour, Sunday Press* 30 August.

Daniel Murphy, *Tolstoy and education, Studies,* winter.

1993   James H. Murphy (ed.), *New beginnings in ministry, Studies*, spring.

Richard Doherty, *Clear the way!: a history of the 38th (Irish) brigade 1941-1947, Sunday Press* 30 May.

Mary E. Daly, *Industrial development and Irish national identity 1922-1939, Studies*, winter.

Robin Neilland, *Walking through Ireland, Sunday Press* 5 December.

1994   Donald Harman Akenson, *The Irish diaspora, Studies*, autumn.

1995   John Laughland, *The death of politics: France under Mitterrand, Sunday Press* 29 January.

Kevin C. Kearns, *Dublin tenement life: an oral history, Studies*, spring.

Proinsias MacAonghusa (ed.), *What Connolly said, Sunday Press* 16 April.

Christopher Frayling, *Strange landscape: a journey through the middle ages, Irish Catholic* 20 July.

David Fitzpatrick, *Oceans of consolation. Personal accounts of Irish migration to Australia, Studies*, winter.

1996   John Coakley and Michael Gallagher (eds.), *Politics in the Republic of Ireland, Studies*, spring.

Aidi Roche, *Children of Chernobyl, Studies*, autumn.

Dáire Keogh, *Edmund Rice 1762-1844, Studies*, winter.

Conor McHale, *Patron of partition: Bishop Thomas Quinlan 1896-1970, Studies*, winter.

1997   Gerard B. Wegemer, *Thomas More: a portrait of courage, Studies*, spring.

Patrick J. Corish, *Maynooth College 1795-1995, Irish Times* 17 June.

Stephen Collins, *The Cosgrave legacy, Studies*, winter.

1998   Patrick Fagan, *Divided loyalties: the question of the oath for Irish Catholics, Studies*, autumn.

Thomas Bartlett, *Theobald Wolfe Tone, Studies*, autumn.

J. L. Hyland, *James Connolly, Studies*, autumn.

Thomas Morrissey, *William Martin Murphy, Studies*, autumn.

Denis Carroll, *Unusual suspects: twelve radical clergymen, The Furrow*, September.

1999   Kevin Donlon, CSSR, *And ink be on their hands, Intercom*, June.

Claus-Ulrich Viol, *Eighteenth-century (sub) versions of stage Irishness, Studies*, summer.

Vincent Ryan, OSB, *The shaping of Sunday and the Eucharist in Irish tradition, Studies*, summer.

Pádraig O'Brien, *Debate aborted 1789-91: Priestly, Paine, Burke and the revolution in France, Studies*, summer.

Oliver P. Rafferty, *The Church, the State and the Fenian threat 1861-75, Studies*, autumn.

Risteárd Mulcahy, *Richard Mulcahy (1886-1971): a family memoir, Studies*, winter.

2000   Edward Daly, *Mister, are you a priest?*, *The Sunday Business Post* 5 November.

2001   Vivienne Belton, *Cardinal Thomas Winning: an authorised biography*, *Irish Catholic*, 1 February.

Liam Swords, *In their own words: the famine in North Connacht 1848-49*, *Studies*, spring.

Daniel Murphy, *A history of Irish emigrant and missionary education*, *Studies*, spring.

Stephen Collins, *The power game: Fianna Fáil Since Lemass*, *Studies*, summer.

Francis Beirne (ed.), *The diocese of Elphin: people, places and pilgrimage*, *Studies*, summer.

T. Ryle Dwyer, *Tans, terror and troubles*, *Sunday Independent* 26 August.

Maria Kelly, *A history of the Black Death in Ireland*, *Studies*, winter.

2002   Martin Tierney, *Sunday thoughts: reflections on every Sunday of the year*, *Irish Catholic* 14 February.

Marcus Tanner, *Ireland's holy wars: the struggle for a nation's soul 1500-2000*, *Studies*, summer.

Paul A. Townend, *Father Mathew, temperance and Irish identity*, *Irish Catholic* 18 July.

Kieran Waldron, *Out of the shadows: emerging secondary schools in the archdiocese of Tuam, 1940-69*, *The Furrow*, September.

Mark Patrick Hederman, *Anchoring the altar: Christianity and the work of art*, *Studies*, autumn.

D

CONTRIBUTIONS TO NEWSPAPERS AND PERIODICALS

1970   'Dublin South-West', *Irish Times* 10 March (drafted for Fifth Years, Good Counsel Secondary School, Mourne Road, Drimnagh).

1974   'Mutiny at Listowel', *Irish Independent* 17 April.

'Publication not futile', *Sunday Press* 21 December.

1976   'Biography of Stack', *Evening Herald* 8 May, *Sunday Press* 9 May, *Irish Press* 11 May, *Kerryman* 25 June.

1977   'History of Garda', *Irish Press* 7 July, *Irish Times* 8 July, *Irish Independent* 13 July.

'Claims that British knew about Rising challenged', *Sunday Independent* 20 November.

1978   'Book launching', *Kerryman* 20 January.

'Biography of Thomas Johnson', *Evening Herald* 18 July, *Irish Press*, *Irish Times* 19 July, *Evening Press* 20 July, *Cork Examiner* 21 July, *Irish Independent* 24 July, *Sunday Press* 6 August.

'Priests' housekeepers', *Irish Press* 22 November.

1979   'Taxing TDs', *Irish Times* 22 June.
'Voting for the scaffold', Irish Press, *Irish Times* 23 July.
'The story of a controversial interview', *Evening Herald* 12 October.
'Big Jim Larkin', *Irish Press* 16 October.
'Britain: the hypocrisy is breathtaking', *Evening Press* 3 December, *Irish Independent* 7 December, *Irish Times* 10 December.

1980   'Book on Thomas O'Donnell', *Irish Independent* 30 May, *Irish Press* 2 June, *Irish Times* 5 June.
'Unchanging message from Belfast', *Irish Press* 7 July, *Irish Independent* 26 July.

1981   'Teampaillín Bán, *Kerryman* 8 May.
'Echoes of Carson', *Sunday Press*, *Sunday Tribune* 1 November, *Irish Times* 23 November.

1982   'Bulgarian history', *Irish Times* 9 August.
'Ireland and Britain', *Irish Press* 20 December, *Irish Times*, 22 December.

1983   'Monsignor O'Rahilly biography', *Irish Times* 26 January, *Cork Examiner* 31 January.
'Castro's Cuba', *Sunday Independent* 17 April.
'De Valera's Watergate', *Sunday Press* 6 November.

1984   'The British Question', *Irish Times* 6 January.
'Cardinal and Sinn Féin', *Irish Press* 21 February.
'Unitary solution', *Sunday Independent* 27 May.
'Ground wasn't large enough', *Sunday Press* 12 August.
'The priest's image', *Irish Press* 27 August.
'The Shroud of Turin', *Intercom*, Dec-Jan 1984-5.

1985   'Australia and G.A.A.', *Irish Press* 8 November, *Irish Times* 9 November.
'The Church and State', *Evening Herald* 19 April, *Irish Independent* 22 April, *Irish Press* 2 May.
'That two sentence letter', *Cork Examiner* 6 August.
'Bilderbeg meeting', *Irish Press* 18 August, *Sunday Independent* 19 August.
'College Opening', *Kerryman* 4 October.
'Blaming the Churches', *Irish Press* 7 October, *Irish Times* 15 October.

1986   'Divorce', *Irish Times* 7 June, *Irish Press* 10 June, *Sunday Independent* 18 June.

1987   'Malicious nonsense', *Irish Press* 26 February, *Sunday Independent*, *Sunday Press* 1 March.
'Role of the laity' (1), *Sunday Press* 14 June, *Irish Times* 16 June, *Irish Independent* 17 June.
'Forests in Finland', *Irish Press* 17 August, *Sunday Independent* 23 August.
'Role of the laity (2)', *Irish Times* 6 October.
'Choosing a new archbishop', *Irish Press* 4 November.

1988 'Stalker-Sampson report on RUC', *Irish Independent* 17 February, *Sunday Press* 19 February.

   'Béal na Bláth, *Irish Times* 30 September.

   'Biased British press', *Sunday Press* 6 November, *Irish Press* 9 November.

1989 'Rushdie, *Irish Independent* 1 March.

   'Michael Collins', *Sunday Press* 2 April.

   'Gorbachev's welcome', *Irish Times* 22 June.

   'Ripe for reform', *Irish Times* 21 August.

   'Is Mr Dukes simply innocent?' *Irish Catholic* 21 August.

   'The Guildford 4', *Irish Times* 27 October.

1990 'Shooting of Collins', *Evening Press*, *Irish Independent* 5 January, *Evening Herald* 15 January.

   'The great O'Rahilly', *Evening Herald* 7 February.

   'Radio priest', *Irish Times* 2 March.

   'Pope's warning on condoms', *Irish Times* 24 September.

1991 'The hard word', *Irish Times* 15 June.

   'Tiresome politics', *Irish Independent* 21 November, *Sunday Press* 24 November, *Irish Times* 25 November.

1992 'Praying for the pope', *Irish Times* 14 August.

   'Orthodox', *Irish Independent* 28 October.

1993 'Article in "Reality"', *Evening Press* 12 January.

   'Talks should be welcomed', *Irish Independent* 9 July.

   'Kerry's football troubles', *Irish Independent* 23 September.

   'British must move', *Sunday Press* 5 December, *Evening Press* 6 December.

1994 'North not democratic', *Sunday Press* 16 January.

   'Mass-going in Ireland', *Irish Times* 6 December.

1999 'A priestly bouquet from Blackrock', *The Brandsma Review*, Feb-March.

2001 'Kerry civil war', *Sunday Independent* 2 September.

2002 'Class of '57 invited to their reunion', *Intercom*, April.

   'Demonised', *Irish News* 10 May.

E

BROADCASTS

1999 RTÉ: Sunday Miscellany: 'Contrasting visits to Poland' 5 December.

2000 RTÉ: Summer lectures: 'James Douglas, concerned citizen', 16 August.

Index of Persons